TEACHING ENGLISH
WITH
INFORMATION TECHNOLOGY

Teaching English with Information Technology

Also available in the Teaching English series:

Teaching English to Young Learners	ISBN 1-898789-13-4
Teaching English One to One	ISBN 1-898789-12-6
Teaching English with Information Technology	ISBN 1-898789-16-9
Lessons in Your Rucksack	ISBN 1-898789-14-2
Guide to English Language Teaching	ISBN 1-898789-15-0

For full details of all our books and our range of magazines for teachers and students, including:

- English Teaching Professional
- Modern English Teacher
- Modern English Digest
- ESL Magazine

Visit our website:
www.KeywaysPublishing.com

TEACHING ENGLISH
WITH
INFORMATION TECHNOLOGY

David Gordon Smith and Eric Baber

Keyways Publishing

Teaching English With Information Technology

Published by:	Keyways Publishing
	PO Box 100, Chichester,
	West Sussex, PO18 8HD, UK
First published by:	Modern English Publishing
Tel:	+44 (0) 1234 576444
Fax:	+44 (0) 1234 576456
Email:	info@KeywaysPublishing.com
Website:	www.KeywaysPublishing.com

© David Gordon Smith and Eric Baber, 2005

All rights reserved. No part of this publication may be reproduced in any form or by any means without the permission of the publishers.

British Library Cataloguing-in-Publication Data

A catalogue record for this book is available from the British Library

ISBN 1-898789-16-9

Design by Navigator Guides

Editor Francesca Collin

Layout by KPL

Printed by Lightning Source, UK

Note: We respect all registered trademarks: all website domain names, site names, software brand names, screenshots and extracts from software products are © by the website owner or publisher named.

Contents

Introduction   7

1	Using Email	15
2	Using Websites for Language Teaching	21
3	WebQuests	40
4	CD-ROMs	49
5	Text-chat, Internet Relay Chat and Instant Messaging	58
6	Using Internet Audio/video-conferencing	70
7	Learning Management Systems	81
8	Creating Your Own Website	89
9	Authoring Software: Creating Interactive Exercises	112
10	Using Standalone Software	121
11	Blogs	140

Appendices

1	Website Addresses	144
2	Language-learning CD-roms	152
3	Books	155
4	Keyboard Shortcuts	156

Glossary   *158*

Index   *176*

Dedications

From David:

    To Sylee

        For her love and support

From Eric:

    To my wife Roisin

        For her faith and love

    To my parents

        For their support and encouragement over the years

Introduction

Who is this book aimed at?

This book is aimed at teachers of English as a foreign or second language (although much will be relevant to teachers of other languages), who wish to incorporate information technology or e-learning into their current practices. Maybe as a teacher you would like to learn how to use websites with your students, or perhaps you're intrigued by the possibilities that video-conferencing offer. Whatever your interests, we won't be assuming any previous experience of using IT to teach English, and we'll be concentrating on how to use the technology to *teach*, not on the technology for its own sake.

We are however assuming a certain minimal amount of experience of working with IT. For example, we'll assume that you are able to switch a computer on, use a mouse, and have probably sent an email, visited a web page and used a word processor at some point in your life. (If you are already feeling out of your depth, then we would suggest you read this book in conjunction with a beginner's guide to computers which will teach you the basics.) On the other hand, if you already have experience in using IT in your teaching, we hope that you will still find something new in this book – perhaps information about a technology you have never worked with, or new ideas about how to use a technology that you are already familiar with.

Introduction

Why use IT in English teaching?

Like many language teachers, you may feel a certain aversion to information technology. "What do I need computers for?" you might ask. After all, you've been teaching English very effectively for years with nothing more technical than a tape recorder or photocopier. You can teach English perfectly well without computers too, surely?

Well, yes, of course you can. But by the same token you can teach English perfectly well without a coursebook, a tape recorder or even a blackboard. However these tools do make life easier and can add a valuable extra dimension to your teaching. Ultimately, computers and the internet are just extra tools in your arsenal - tools which can open up whole new vistas within your teaching practice.

As well as simply wanting to learn how to use new tools, you might have other reasons for wanting to incorporate IT into your teaching:

- you work for an organisation such as the British Council or a university where IT skills are important for your career;
- your location prevents you from teaching English face-to-face;
- you're starting to feel a bit stale and need something to re-awaken your interest in teaching;
- you're a freelance teacher and want to make yourself more employable by increasing your range of skills;
- your students have asked your advice on how they can use technology to enhance their learning, or have asked you to incorporate IT in your teaching;
- you're simply curious about these important new developments in our field.

What are the advantages of using IT?

Incorporating information technology into your teaching practice can bring many concrete benefits. To illustrate them, let's take a look at some example case studies.

Case study 1 - Maria

Maria is a Brazilian teacher of English in a small town in the interior of Brazil. Her teenage students have never met a native speaker of English. Maria has never been to an English-speaking country and feels insecure about her own English, as well as being aware that she is not up-to-date with recent methodological developments. The textbooks she is told to use are out-of-date and not relevant to the students' lives.

Information technology can help her alleviate all these problems. Using the internet, she can enable her students to interact with American teenagers using text chat. She can keep up-to-date with developments in ELT through reading online journals, visiting the websites of professional organisations such as TESOL or IATEFL, and attending online conferences. She can improve her own English through a language exchange with a native English speaker who wants to learn Portuguese. She can use resources on the internet to check if language is correct, and ask colleagues online about tricky grammar points that she herself is not sure about. She can use material from websites to prepare up-to-date and relevant lessons for her students, or even download ready-made lessons which she only has to photocopy. The internet supports and empowers Maria in her own teaching. Best of all, none of the online resources described above require a particularly powerful computer or fast internet connection.

Case study 2 - Stuart

Stuart is a highly-qualified native speaker teacher of English who has taught in various countries for many years. He also writes and edits teaching materials on a freelance basis for different educational publishers. For personal reasons he and his family have settled in a small town in the north of Scotland. Stuart's partner works full-time and they have a young daughter who Stuart looks after for most of the day. The nearest conventional language school is more than a hundred miles away.

IT enables Stuart to pursue his career even in such a remote location. Using ▶

▶ the internet, Stuart can teach clients living in different countries using audio- and video-conferencing. He has the flexibility to work at the times that suit him, leaving him free to spend time with his daughter. He doesn't need to leave the house, and can even teach in his pyjamas, should he wish. He can continue to work for publishers, sending in his work and keeping in touch using email and conferencing. He can also design his own website to advertise his services, and keep in touch with his friends and colleagues around the world using text-chat software. He can even gain additional qualifications using internet-enabled distance learning. IT and the internet give Stuart the flexibility to live wherever he likes and still work.

Case study 3 – Gertrud

Gertrud is a human resources manager at a medium-sized German company. The company does a lot of business with the USA and the employees desperately need language training. However, not only do the employees not have time for regular classes, the company cannot afford to pay for face-to-face training for all its employees.

As a solution, Gertrud organises regular one-day seminars with a Business English trainer for different groups of employees. These seminars are complemented using a content management system on the company intranet, which the employees use between seminars. Employees can do language exercises involving listening, reading, vocabulary and grammar work. They can write texts which are sent to the trainer via email and then corrected and returned. Gertrud and the trainer can keep track of individual students' progress using the system, as well as seeing how much time each student is dedicating to learning English. In addition, those employees who only need to correspond in English are given translation software to help them understand the letters and emails they receive. A web page on the company intranet gives them useful company-specific phrases to use in correspondence. Should they wish, they can have outgoing correspondence checked by the English trainer, who has arranged to proofread and return any correspondence by email within a 24-hour period. The whole package works out cheaper in both time and money for the company and for the employees.

To conclude, IT can empower you as a teacher and improve your teaching for the following reasons:

1. It provides access to up-to-date material on every imaginable topic.
2. It makes transferring straightforward information very simple, potentially allowing you to spend classroom time more meaningfully.
3. It can help you create exercises and materials that are easily reusable, thereby saving you time in the long run.
4. It renders geographical distance less significant or even insignificant.
5. It can be cheaper than face-to-face teaching.
6. It allows non-native speakers to interact with native speakers.
7. It allows students to study at their own pace, whenever they want.
8. It enables people living far apart to come together and form communities.
9. It can be intrinsically motivating and fun.

One last point - despite what some teachers might claim, computers are unlikely to do us out of a job for quite a while to come (although they could arguably do so one day). Most people these days see IT as something which complements traditional teaching, rather than replacing it. Many people would argue that there is some special, even magical which is found when people come together in person to learn a language - a quality which is very hard to replicate using IT.

How to use this book

This book is organised into chapters based around individual topics. You can read it cover to cover, or you might want to simply dip into the chapters which appeal to you. The more accessible technologies are near the start of the book, with the technologies requiring a steeper learning curve towards the end - but don't let that stop you from skipping from section to section as you please. Our approach is the following: rather than telling you all about what a particular technology actually is, we give you practical ideas on how to use it. After all, you don't need to understand the underlying principles of the internet in order to be able to visit a web page - one reason why the internet is as useful as it is. Our aim is to give you ideas which you can take away and use on Monday morning in class, as well as hopefully inspiring you to carry out longer-term projects.

A word on website addresses

If you have any experience of using the internet at all, you'll know that it is notoriously fluid and changeable. Of course, this dynamism is part of the internet's attraction, but it leads to problems when writing or using a book about IT; websites which were receiving thousands of hits last month may be just a pleasant memory today.

To help minimise the number of "404 Page Not Found" error messages you have to deal with, there are no website addresses in the body of the book. Instead, they are all in the separate Appendix, which can more easily be kept up to date. Any name you see underlined in the text (like Google) has a web address listed in the Appendix. An up-to-date version of the Appendix can be found on the Modern English Publishing website – if an address in the appendix doesn't work, take a look at www.modernenglishpublishing.com for the current version.

Some IT basics

We said earlier in this introduction that we weren't going to try and teach you all about computers. But there are a few terms which we think are worthwhile clarifying right at the start, as well as a few tips you may find useful. You can find a more extensive Glossary at the back of this book. So, at the risk of blinding you with science, here are some IT basics.

A computer **network** consists of two or more computers linked together. This allows them to exchange information. The **internet** is the largest computer network in the world, and in fact is made up of many smaller networks. (By the way, in this book we write internet with a lowercase initial letter, as we're guessing that over time this will become the accepted spelling, in the same way that words like 'telephone' and 'television' which were once capitalised no longer are.)

Contrary to popular belief, the **world wide web** (or **WWW** or simply **web**) is, strictly speaking, not synonymous with the internet. The web is a part of the internet and consists of **websites**, which in turn consist of **web pages**. Web pages and websites are linked together using **hyperlinks**, which allow the user to jump from one page to another with a simple click. (If you've used the web at all, you will have already encountered hyperlinks – they're the underlined words or images which you click on to take you to another page within the same website, or a different website completely.)

In order to visit websites you use a piece of software called a **browser**, such as Netscape Navigator, Internet Explorer or Opera. Websites are often found by typing their **address** or **URL** (uniform resource locator; for example our URL is www.modernenglishpublishing.com) into the browser. The website address will usually consist of www. followed by the company's **domain name**; in the previous example, the domain name would be modernenglishpublishing.com. Another way of accessing websites is via a **search engine**, which is a special website where you can search for websites on a particular topic by entering specific keywords.

Email is another use of the internet, and allows people to send electronic documents to each other, provided that the sender knows the recipient's **email address**. Note that an email address is not the same as a website address. An email address normally looks something like john.smith@modernenglishpublishing.com while a website address normally looks like www.modernenglishpublishing.com. Email addresses again use the domain name but this time preceded by a person's name and the @ symbol, rather than the www. found in a website address.

E-learning is a term which is difficult to pin down, but is generally agreed to mean using information technology in some way to teach or learn. A **blended solution** involves combining e-learning with **face-to-face** (sometimes written **F2F**) teaching.

Finally, the more you use your computer, the more you will find **keyboard shortcuts** handy. Many functions for which you currently use your mouse can also be performed using the keyboard, provided you know the right combinations of keys to press. In Appendix 4 we have listed a number of the

Introduction

most frequently used keyboard shortcuts. These will save you time, and may well help reduce the risk of acquiring RSI (Repetitive Strain Injury) which can sometimes be brought on by frequent use of the mouse.

Let's get started

We hope this introduction has helped give you an overview of what the book contains and what it is meant to achieve.

So now, without further ado, let's get started!

Chapter 1

Using Email

Email is one of the simplest tools available to the language teacher interested in e-learning. Most people already use email as part of their daily life and have email software installed on their computers. Email is usable with just about any computer and there are seldom any problems with the technology.

If you don't already have email, the easiest way to get an email account is by opening a free web-based email account with a website such as Hotmail or Yahoo. With this approach, you go to a website and log on with a user name and password (which you create the first time you visit the website). You can then check to see if you have received any emails since you last logged on, and you can compose new emails to send to other people.

The main disadvantage of such web-based email accounts is that you generally need to be online to write emails, which could be expensive for those of us who like to write lengthy emails or simply need more time to think. One way round this is to write your text in a word processor while offline, then copy and paste it into the appropriate window on the website after going online and logging into your email account. Having said that, you can now use Hotmail addresses offline using Microsoft's free email software Outlook Express, so there are other ways around spending ages online.

So how can you use email with your students? Let's look at a few of the many possibilities.

1
Using Email

Homework and feedback by email

Probably the simplest way to incorporate email into your teaching is to set your students homework via email. This homework can then be corrected in class, or alternatively students could return their work via email, with you then sending them feedback also by email.

The homework could be in the form of a writing task, or exercises such as gap-fills or matching exercises. You could include the homework directly in the text of the email (probably the easiest option) or write it in Word or another word processor and send it as an attachment. If you're feeling adventurous, you could also send pictures, audio files, or even web pages as email attachments as part of the homework. Bear in mind, though, that many people get nervous about receiving email attachments, as they can contain viruses. Make sure you give your email a relevant subject line so that the recipient knows you mean no harm. Also check the size of your attachment (usually shown automatically by your email program). Anything over 100 kilobytes or so may irritate the recipient, due to the length of time needed to download it. Large attachments (one megabyte or over) are often simply rejected by the receiver's email account, particularly with web-based email accounts such as Hotmail, so it's best to avoid them.

Student activities

Email story-writing: Get your students to use email to work on exercises and tasks together. For example, you can ask them to write a story collaboratively: the first student writes the first line, then emails it on to the second student, who writes the second line and sends it to the next student, and so on. Such an activity does need to be planned beforehand (for example, you need to determine the order of the students, and make sure students will log in regularly to pass the exercise on) but with sufficient planning it can work very well.

Information-gathering: Set students a task (this can be a larger-scale project) for which they will need to gather various items of information, at least some of which will require them to email companies or other institutions for relevant information. This might include gathering facts or figures, prices, terms and conditions and more. The students should have to process the information and produce some kind of output - this could be for example a PowerPoint presentation which they then email to you.

Jigsaw activities and role-plays: These can work similarly to activities you might use in the classroom, but probably more effectively, since students don't have any visual clues to help them. Email each student a different piece of information as well as a task which requires them to find out information from another class member. For example, two students might be potential buyers of a product, while three other students are suppliers. The buyers have to email the suppliers with questions regarding price, delivery time and so on. Negotiations might be allowed, increasing the flow of email activity. Many classroom activities can easily be transferred to email and can be even more productive via this medium.

Proofreading students' documents

Many students need to write texts in English, whether business emails, academic papers or newspaper articles. Get students to send you texts by email for you to proofread and return. If you're feeling entrepreneurial you could even charge for the service – why not advertise your services on your website?

Keeping students informed

You can use emails to keep students informed on a wide range of issues such as: English-language films on TV or in the cinema you'd recommend; relevant news items in a newspaper or on a news website. In the latter case, you can send them the website address and ask them to read it before the next lesson, in which case you can base the lesson on the article; a play in English that is on at the moment in your area; other events in your area that your students might find of interest and which will take place before you see them again.

Email discussion groups

There are very many email discussion groups that both you and your students can join. An email discussion group or list is normally devoted to a single topic, such as Elvis, banjo-playing or reasons why one should hate Microsoft. (The whole of life's rich pageant is reflected in the topics for which email discussion groups exist.)

Once you have joined an email discussion group (usually free), you will be told a single email address to which you can send emails. Any emails you send to this address are then forwarded to all the members on the list; similarly, you will receive emails from anyone else on the list who has sent an email to that address. A group can have a membership of a dozen people or several thousand. Groups can either be moderated or unmoderated – with a moderated group each email is checked for interest and relevancy before being passed on to the group members. In an unmoderated group no such checking takes place.

A good place to start is YahooGroups. Yahoo groups are easy to join and use, and there are several teaching-related groups, such as the one devoted to Scott Thornbury's ideas on "Teaching Unplugged". You could encourage your students to join groups they are interested in and make contributions in English. You could join the same groups and give them feedback on their emails (privately, of course!).

If you are feeling adventurous you could even set up your own email group (easy to do with Yahoo groups). For example, you could create one for a particular group of students so that you can communicate with each other between classes.

Netiquette

A word of warning regarding email discussion groups: be careful not to infringe netiquette (internet etiquette). There are many rules of conduct related to email groups, which the newbie (new user/member) is normally unaware of. For example, it is considered bad form when replying to a previous posting to send your reply to the whole group, when your reply is only of interest to the person who wrote the original message. The best idea is to 'lurk' for a while when you join a new group – this involves reading other people's messages without contributing your own, until you are familiar with the culture of a particular group.

Similarly, most groups have an archive of previous messages – it's best to consult this archive before posting, to make sure your question or comment has not already appeared on the list. For further tips on netiquette a good place to start is Arlene Rinaldi's <u>The Net: User Guidelines and Netiquette</u> (see Appendix 1 for website address). While the rules outlined there may not be applicable to all email groups, they will give you a good idea of the sort of thing to watch out for.

Managing your emails

Depending on the size and degree of enthusiasm of a group it may generate very few emails, or tens or even hundreds a day. While this can be exciting and very useful, it can also mean that you may need to implement some system to manage your emails. One useful mechanism is the following. Create a folder in your email program called, for example, 'Elvis email group'. Then check out your email program for a functionality called 'Inbox Assistant', 'Message Rules' or something similar. Using that functionality you can filter all emails from a particular list into the folder you created for it. For example, you can set it up in such a way that any emails sent to elvis@yahoogroups.com are moved directly into the Elvis list folder. Doing this for any email lists you join can help you manage your mail more efficiently – some days you may want to go through everything in detail, while other days you may want to just glance at the discussions as they take place.

Conclusion

Email is a tool worth investigating if:
- you want to use a technology which is trouble-free and familiar to most people;
- you or your students have limited technical resources, or do not want to learn to use a new technology;
- you want something to complement face-to-face teaching, e.g. by setting homework by email;
- you want to proofread students' texts;
- real-time online communication is not important.

Chapter 2

Using Websites for Language Teaching

Most people have some experience with visiting websites, and the World Wide Web constitutes an incredible resource to use with your students. In many cases you can adapt online materials for use with activities and exercise-types you've been using for years. However, the medium also lends itself to new and different activities. Before we look at specific examples of tasks you can set your students, though, let's take a look at some strategies for sifting through the overwhelming amount of material on the web.

Using a search engine

The secret to finding good resources on the web is being able to use a search engine effectively. A list of recommended search engines can be found in Appendix 1. At the time of writing, the best search engine is commonly considered to be Google, although competitors such as AllTheWeb are gaining ground.

To use a search engine, you simply enter one or more keywords or 'search terms' into a box on the web page, then click on a button marked 'search' or similar. (In this book, example search terms to typ in are in `Courier` font.)

For example, if you wanted to find information on Australia, you might start by simply entering the word `Australia` into the box then clicking on search.

Generally when using a search engine, the more keywords you enter, the better your results will be – they will certainly be more refined. With some search engines, you can specify if you want to find pages which contain all the keywords or only some, by using the operators 'and' and 'or'.

For example, if you want to find pages which contain both the words 'vocabulary' and 'grammar', you would type the following into the search window:

> `vocabulary AND grammar`

If you wanted to find pages, which contained either one of the terms or both terms, you would enter the following:

> `vocabulary OR grammar`

It's often useful to search for a specific phrase rather than individual keywords. To do this, you normally put the phrase into quotation marks. For example, if you wanted to find a page with grammar exercises, doing a search for

> `'grammar exercises'`

would probably give you better results than searching for

> `grammar AND exercises`

Normally you can also exclude words from your search by putting a minus sign (-) before the word. This can be very useful if one of your search terms has more than one meaning. Let's say you want to find information on the Buddhist concept of nirvana. If you simply do a search for the word 'nirvana' you will likely turn up many pages on the rock band Nirvana, as well as on Buddhism. You can dramatically improve your results simply by excluding (for example) the words 'rock' and 'music' from your search, i.e. by entering the following as your search terms:

> `nirvana -rock -music`

Probably the best results will be obtained by searching for the following terms:

> `nirvana AND Buddhism  - rock - music`

Be aware that every search engine differs slightly in the way it treats search terms. For example, Google automatically searches for pages which contain all your keywords, so there is no point trying to use the AND and OR operators with it. Search engines generally have a page of tips which help you search more efficiently; these tips are normally worth reading. Look for a link called 'search tips' or similar on the search engine home page.

Copyright on the internet

All the material available on the web is copyright. Using copyrighted material in your classes will probably not cause you any problems, but be aware that you should not publish your exercises in any form (including on your own website) without having obtained permission from the copyright holder. Website owners do not have to declare that their materials are copyright - they automatically are! Let's now go on to see what EFL/TESOL websites have to offer and what exercises and topics are available.

EFL/TESOL websites, and forums

Probably the most obvious web-based resources for teaching are those websites devoted to teaching English. These tend to have been created either by language schools (in some cases the schools themselves are entirely online) or dedicated individuals. Some sites charge for access, most (at the time of writing) don't. The sites themselves often include interactive exercises, where students, for example, choose the correct multiple-choice answer and then check their answers by clicking on a button to receive instant feedback. Another popular tool is the discussion forum, where teachers or students can post messages which other people can read and reply to.

> **Jargon box**
> In a discussion forum, a sequence comprising the original message plus all the replies and counter-replies is known as a 'thread'.

This all sounds wonderful in theory, but as so often on the internet, there are snags. Possibly the best, and simultaneously the worst, thing about the web is the fact that anyone is theoretically able to publish their work. This means that any teacher can produce their own language exercises, and the quality of the materials available reflects this fact. Some exercises could be considered methodologically unsound, and sometimes the language is simply incorrect.

Another problem (which applies to using computers for language teaching in general) is the fact that computers see things very much in black and white, whereas language on the other hand is notoriously fuzzy. This fundamental incompatibility means that it is very difficult to design exercises which will accept all possible answers for a particular question. (This is one reason why multiple-choice questions are so popular for online exercises.) The result of this is that the poor unsuspecting student may, for example, type in the sentence "Can I help you?" as an answer to a question and be told it is invalid, simply because the computer was programmed to accept only "May I help you?"

Discussion forums provide students and teachers with a chance to air their views, but often turn into soapboxes or even boxing rings. Be sure to warn your students about the negative reactions they might experience to their postings.

From a student's point of view, probably the major drawback is that the language they produce on the forum is never corrected. To get around this problem, you might want to recommend your students that they contribute to a specific forum of your choice, which will enable you to correct their messages in class or by email.

Exercises and activities

In our opinion, where the web really comes into its own for the EFL teacher is as a resource for planning lessons. No other medium offers such an enormous range of material on every conceivable topic (and not a few inconceivable ones). And this material is already in electronic form, making it simplicity itself to copy and paste texts into a word processor, ready for being made into exercises.

Here are some suggestions for ways to use websites to create (almost) instant exercises.

Gap-fills

Find a text of interest to your students, then remove words from your chosen text to make a simple gap-fill exercise (you will first need to copy the text from the web page and paste it into a text-editing program). Choose whether you want to give the students the missing words (which makes the exercise easier) or if they have to guess the words without any help. You might want to focus on collocations (words which occur together), for example verb + noun combinations. Remember to number the gaps to make correction easier.

Word-completion

Use the 'search and replace' function in your word processor to remove the vowels from a text. Do this by searching for each vowel in turn, and replacing it with an asterisk '*' or an underscore '_'. (It's a good idea to put a space after the asterisk or underscore in the 'replace' box, which will make the text easier to read.) Students then have to write in the missing vowels.

Reconstructing text

An alternative is to use the search and replace function to remove all the spaces from the text (put a single space into the 'search' box, leave the 'replace' box blank, then click on 'replace all'). Students have to split the text into individual words.

'Cracking the code'

Put a text into 'code' simply by changing the font for your text into a pictorial font like Wingdings in Windows. (You can change the font in Microsoft Word by highlighting a piece of text, pressing Ctrl+D and then selecting the desired font from the list given.) Tell students which letters two or three of the symbols stand for (E and T are a good choice) and let them work out the rest for themselves. You might want to print out a separate worksheet with a list of the symbols used. Students write the corresponding letter next to each symbol as they crack the code, e.g.

code	plain text
♎	
♦	t
&	k
☐	
♋	a

Make sure you yourself have a note of which symbol corresponds to which letter!

Reading comprehension

Visit a website you think will interest your students (or ask them to recommend one). Find a continuous text appropriate for their level and copy and paste it into a word processor. Write comprehension and/or discussion questions related to the text. You may want to simplify the language of the text if necessary. You can also select key vocabulary to pre-teach, or provide a glossary or translations of difficult terms.

Jigsaw reading

Print out several different texts from the same website and give a different one to each student in the class. Students read their texts and tell the other students what they've read about, using their own words. Students can also prepare questions related to their text for the other students, or check new vocabulary in their dictionaries and teach it to their partners.

Information gap

Students work in pairs. Give one student in the pair a printout of a text with elements of the information removed (e.g. names of people or places) and give another student the same text with other elements removed. Each then reads through their text and gives the other one the missing information, which that student writes into the gaps in his or her text. Students can ask each other appropriate questions to elicit the information; you may want to supply prompts to help them formulate suitable questions.

Topics

Depending on the interests of your students (and yours of course!) you can find information on absolutely any topic under the sun on the web, and turn it into exercises such as the ones described above. Here are a few example topics to get you started, along with a few specific ideas for activities; between the topics below and the exercise-types above you will be able to create dozens of tasks for your students.

Music

Using the A – Z Lyrics site or by doing a Google search (search for "*name of song*" *lyrics*, putting quotation marks around the song title to ensure that the search engine looks for the whole title instead of the individual words), find the lyrics to one of your or your students' favourite song. (Note that sometimes the lyrics on websites have been typed out by someone – not necessarily a native speaker – listening to the recording and writing down what they think the words are, so exercise discretion when looking for lyrics to use.)

Here are some ideas for activities using song lyrics:
- Turn the song into a gap-fill listening exercise (see above).
- Ask students to write an extra verse to the song.
- Re-write the lyrics so that some of the lines are wrong – students listen to the song and have to correct the lyrics.
- Put the lines into the wrong order – students have to put them in the correct order. (You could jumble up the lyrics from two different songs to make this more difficult.)
- Make a lyrics quiz by taking lines from several different

songs and reading them out – students have to identify which song they come from.
- Students (possibly in groups) produce a "video" to the song, which they then act out as you play the song (naturally this works best if the song relates a narrative).

Celebrities and famous people

Most students (especially younger ones) are interested in celebrities like pop musicians or film actors. This interest in celebrities is also shared by the thousands of people who make up fan websites; a search for the name of an actor such as Harrison Ford will turn up thousands of hits, many of which will be home-made fan sites. (Note that the language on some home-made sites may not conform to your idea of correct English - if you find this unacceptable you will have to choose sites with care. Alternatively, you can use mistakes as a basis for discussion in class.)

- Get your students to search for information about their favourite stars and then tell each other about them.
- Get students to work in groups to make quizzes for each other. Fan sites are great for celebrity trivia. Questions could be for example "What is Tom Cruise's favourite food?" or "What does Madonna do to keep fit?"
- Prepare your own quiz in advance by doing a little bit of research on the web. Give the quiz to your students as a worksheet; the students search for the answers on the web. You could follow this up with a role-play where one person is the celebrity and the other is a journalist asking them questions about the topics which were featured in the quiz.

Biography.com features biographies of famous and not-so-famous people, both living and dead. Simply type the name of the person into the search box and the website will show you that person's biography.

- Use the site to find extra information about people featured in the course book you are using (or assign this task to students, perhaps for homework).
- Copy and paste a biography into a word processor. Remove the name of the person from the text. Students read the text and try to work out who the text refers to.

- Give the students a text about a particular person to read. In pairs they role-play an interview between a journalist and the person.
- Give each student a text about a different person. The student then takes on the role of that person. Students ask each other yes/no questions to find out who each person is, e.g. "Are you alive?", "Are you a politician?" etc.
- Take a text about a person who your students will be familiar with, and alter some of the facts in the text. Students have to correct your changes. They could do the necessary research on the internet if you have access in the classroom.

Other good websites about celebrities are Hello! and the BBC's Music Profiles pages.

Film and music reviews

There are many websites which feature reviews of current films or music. Two good sources of information about films, including reviews, are the Internet Movie Database and the All Movie Guide, whose sister site the All Music Guide provides information about music. Naturally this content will appeal to most students (especially younger ones) although you might find the language needs simplifying for the texts to be usable. Note also that some websites may contain strong language or slang.

- Get students to ask each other which films they have seen, or which CDs they have bought, recently. Students find reviews for these films or CDs on the internet (just search for 'name of film/CD + review' in a search engine) and say if they agree with the review or not.
- Remove the name of the film and actors/CD title and musicians from the review. (Simply copy and paste the review into a word processor and replace the specific names with XXXXXX.) The students read the review and try to guess which film/CD it refers to.

Again, many of these sites have forums that students can contribute to, giving their opinion of the films or CDs in question.

Astrology & star signs

The internet is full of astrology websites like <u>Astrology.com</u>. **Caution**: these can be a lot of fun, but be aware that students with strong religious views may be offended by astrology.
- Send your students to the site to research their star signs, or the other students' star signs. Do they agree with what the sites say?
- Print out texts describing different star signs, having removed any references to the signs themselves in the texts. The students should interview each other to find out which texts fit best to which people. At the end students should reveal their signs, and you tell students which signs the texts refer to. Do they match up?
- Print out predictions for the coming week, for all signs. Keep them until the week is past. Ask students what they did during that week. Show them the now-superseded predictions and ask the students if the predictions correspond to what they actually did. Alternatively, get students to write retrospective predictions for the week which has past, and compare them to the real predictions.

Food

Food is a topic which few people can fail to be interested in, and the profusion of food-related sites on the internet reflects this. As well as many sites devoted to recipes, you can find sites explaining healthy eating and nutrition.
- Ask students what their favourite foods are. Send students online to find recipes for their favourite foods (or find recipes yourself if students don't have internet access). Students read recipes and explain how to make the dishes to each other.
- Find a recipe for a dish which students will be familiar with. (Just search for ' `(name of dish) + recipe`' in a search engine like Google.) Blank out significant words

such as names of ingredients. Can students guess what the recipe is for?
- Alternatively, put the recipe steps into the wrong order – can students find the correct order? Mix steps from two recipes together to make this more difficult.
- Tweak a recipe so that it includes deliberate mistakes. (There is plenty of scope for humour here.) Can students correct the mistakes?
- Get students to write down everything that they ate yesterday (or what they eat on a typical day). Students then use a nutrition website such as Calorie Control Council to work out how many calories they consumed. Is their calorie consumption appropriate for their age/sex etc? **Caution**: be very wary of using this activity if you know or suspect that any of your students may have eating disorders.
- If you are talking about a particular country (perhaps one featured in the course book), use the internet to find information about typical dishes from that country. (Search for '(name of country) + food' or '(name of country) + typical + food' in a search engine.) You could print out information about typical dishes from several countries and get students to guess which countries they come from.
- Tell students they are going to go on a trip to (for example) London. Get them to use the internet to find restaurants (perhaps for a particular type of cuisine such as Sri Lankan or Mongolian) in London. They have to choose which restaurant they would prefer to eat at. Some restaurant web pages allow you to book tables online. While we don't recommend that you get students to fraudulently book tables under fictitious names, you could get students to go through the motions of booking without actually carrying it through. Of course, if a particular student is really going on holiday to a particular city, you could certainly get them to book a table for real. There is also no reason why students couldn't write an email to a particular restaurant with an enquiry, such as asking if they cater for vegetarians.

Using Websites for Language Teaching

- The internet is certainly the easiest way to find restaurant menus from other countries. Search for `menu + restaurant` to get you started – add the name of a particular country, city, or cuisine if you want to be more specific. For example, searching for 'menu Italian restaurant Edinburgh' in Google will yield links to websites about Italian restaurants in Edinburgh, including menus. These menus can be used as realia for role-plays, for reading comprehension, or for a cross-cultural discussion. You could search for menus in different cities to compare the cost of eating out. Alternatively, find menus from different restaurants in the same city, and ask students in groups to decide which restaurant they would prefer to eat at. You could allocate them a budget and ask them to decide which dishes they would order.

Jobs

One of the great advantages of the internet is the easy access it allows you to authentic resources, job advertisements being a case in point. Real, current, job advertisements for real jobs are fantastic material to use with your students – sites like <u>Totaljobs</u> will always have several hundred up-to-date jobs advertisements.

- Find a selection of job advertisements which are relevant to your students. (Search for `(job title)+job advertisements` in a search engine.) Students should decide which job they are best qualified for. You could ask students to write a version of their CV specific to that application and write a cover letter. Why not get your students to really send their CVs and cover letter to the contact person named in the advertisement? The worst thing that can happen is they will be asked to come for an interview!
- Find different job ads on the internet and remove the name of the positions. Students read the ads and guess which jobs the ads refer to.

- With advanced students, you could find job advertisements from different countries e.g. the US and UK. Students compare the job ads and see how they differ. What conclusions can the students draw about differences between the respective cultures?

Holidays

Holidays are a favourite topic in most English classes (and coursebooks), and the internet has an enormous amount of resources related to travel.

- Tell your students they are going on holiday to, for example, the USA. They have to plan an itinerary by finding out information about different places in the country and choosing where they would like to visit. You should probably give the students a few relevant links to get them started. This idea can easily be developed into a full-blown WebQuest (see Chapter 3 on WebQuests for more details).
- Ask your students to make a presentation on a place they have visited by finding information about it on the internet.
- Many tourist destinations have sites with webcams showing the beach or other sights at all times of the day. Get students to find a webcam site for a place they have visited. (Search for '(name of place)+webcam' in a search engine.) They should tell the other students about the resort using the webcam images as a prompt.
- Students can use the internet to check what the weather is like for a place they have visited, or will visit, using a site like weather.com. If the whole class has just come back from holiday, or is about to go on holiday, then students could find out which is the hottest/coldest destination.

History

There are some great history sites available such as The History Channel and The History Channel UK. These contain texts as well as audio and video recordings about many phases of history so you are likely to find content to interest both youngsters and adults.

- Many history websites include timelines. Make an information gap activity for pair work by copying and pasting a timeline into Microsoft Word. Make a worksheet for each student in the pair. Student A has half the information for the timeline, and student B has the other half. Students have to ask each other questions to complete their timeline.
- Make a quiz about the history of students' home towns or countries. Search for "(name of town/country) + history" to get you started.
- Get students to prepare their own quizzes on the history of their country.
- Copy a text into a word processor and insert deliberate mistakes into the history. Students have to find the mistakes.
- On The History Channel website you can also find a This Day In History section; this allows a student to find out what happened in the field of entertainment, automotive, or general interest and more on their birthday. They can read through the information they find most interesting and report back to the rest of the class.
- Alternatively, you can allocate a different student every week to find out the most interesting thing that happened that week in history. That student can then spend 10 minutes every day reading about that day in history, and on Friday can then tell the rest of the class about the most interesting event they've read about.
- You can also combine topics, such as music and history – using the This Day in Rock & Roll History site you can use tasks from either the music or the history topics.

Poetry

The web is an ideal place to find poetry resources. Everything from classical poems, to contemporary poetry, to poetry for children is available, generally for free.

- Copy and paste a poem into a word processor. Take out the

rhyming words – students have to work out what the missing words are. Give the students the missing words (in the wrong order) to make it easier.
- Copy a poem into a word processor and mix up the order of the lines. Students have to put the words into the right order. Mix lines from two different poems together to make it more challenging.
- Alternatively, take out certain sections of the poem (perhaps the second halves of certain lines) and ask the students to come up with their own ideas about how to complete the poem. Get the class to vote for the best suggestions, and then show them the original.
- Find a selection of poems and give them to your students. The students rate the poems and choose their favourites.
- If you have internet access in the classroom, give the students a topic (perhaps related to the current course book topic) and get them to find an appropriate poem on the internet.

News

Naturally, news websites like the BBC or CNN are a great resource for teachers of English. There you can find articles and often audio or video files reporting on the latest news. These are easily used in class as resources (although audio and video take a bit more effort – see Chapter 10 on using standalone software for more information).

Using news websites you could:
- Send students to the website for homework – each person has to find a news story which interests them and tell the class about it. Or print out different news stories and use them as the basis for a jigsaw reading activity (see above).
- Take a current issue and get students to investigate it on different news websites – how does the reporting differ? For this, it's probably best to choose news sites which generally have radically different views, such as (in Britain) The Guardian and The Times. You don't need to restrict yourself to UK news websites, though – try

international ones, as long as they are in English.
- Many news sites have forums where visitors can express their opinions on the issues featured – a perfect opportunity for students to use their English in the real world. Make sure you give them feedback on their contributions to the forums.
- Often news websites have email newsletters, where they send you an email every day with the latest headlines. Get your students to sign up for a week. In class you could show them selected headlines and ask them to explain what the story was about. Or focus on the language used in the headlines, maybe by making a gap-fill exercise using the headlines or by playing 'Hangman' with the headlines.

Explanations

How Stuff Works is a popular American website that explains, well, how stuff works. Have you ever wondered how a photocopier works? How Stuff Works will provide the answer, in language which any lay person can understand, but while still providing enough detail to keep the more technically-minded happy. It features plenty of diagrams – often animated – which help you to understand the explanations. This great resource works especially well with Technical English classes, but will also appeal to any students who have a little bit of curiosity about the world.

- Let's say you have a text in your course book about the man who invented the biro pen (Mr Biro, as it happens) – send your students to How Stuff Works to find out how it works.
- Print out a text from How Stuff Works and give each student in a group one page so that they have to exchange their knowledge in order to figure out the whole thing.
- Send one group to find out (for example) how air bags work, another to learn about fuel gauges, and a third to investigate anti-lock brakes. Each group then has to make a presentation to the class explaining their particular technology. One tip – get students to copy the diagrams from the site to make into handouts or slides for the

presentation. (You can copy a picture from a website in Windows simply by right-clicking on it and choosing the 'save' option.)
- Ask students to find out how something works, and then describe it to the rest of the class without telling them what the object is. The rest of the class has to guess what is being described.

Company websites

Some of the most professional websites on the web are those belonging to companies, for whom the internet is an increasingly important marketing and organisational resource. Naturally company websites are particularly relevant to Business English teaching, but General English learners will often also be interested in particular companies (for example household names such as Nike or The Body Shop).

- Often course books feature specific companies or business celebrities – get students to visit the company's websites to find out more.
- If you're teaching at a company, visit the company website for texts to use in class (often students are surprised by what they learn – few people bother to look at their own company's website). Texts from a competitor's website are often even more motivating for students – everyone in business is interested in what the competition is up to.
- Some company websites have presentations which you can download. Students give the presentations in class. This is often particularly interesting with competitor's presentations.
- Prepare a quiz with questions relating to a particular company (possibly the students' own). Students visit the company's website to find the answers.

Sports

Many students are interested in sports, no matter what age they are. Whatever type of sport they're interested in there's bound to be something on the web – the BBC Sports section has up-to-date information about football (soccer), tennis, golf, horse-racing and lots more. With the information available on that and other sites you can:

- Give students a handout containing questions for which they need to find the answers on the site (such as "Who won the league in 2003?", "Who came last?", "What clubs were relegated in 2000?" etc).
- Ask each student to track one player or one team over a period of time. At the end of that time each student has to write a small report to hand in to you, or a presentation to give to the other students, describing how well the player or team did.
- Have students compare information about different, competing clubs or individuals. Have them find out when a club was formed, how much money has been invested in it in the past 5 years, how many times the team-members have been exchanged and so on. Groups of students can either find out all the information, or different groups gather different information and then exchange their findings orally.

Other useful sites are <u>Soccernet</u>, <u>The Guardian's</u> football pages, and the <u>Central Directory for English Soccer on the Net</u>.

Romance and Dating

Depending on your students' age and cultural background, romance and dating websites can be lots of fun. Different sites operate differently; some allow you to view other people's profiles for free, while others allow you to set up your own profile at no cost. One that offers both (in a limited way) is <u>DatingDirect</u>. Here are a few ideas for ways of exploiting such sites with your students:

- Ask your students to write a description of their perfect partner. They then go to the site and see if they can find a match based on the most number of similarities.
- In pairs, students write a description of what they consider to be the other student's perfect partner (without asking them any information first). They then compare ideas, confirming whether they agree or not! They then go online

and find a person that matches the description.
- Ask students to write a description of themselves as if they were going to post it to the website (though they may not actually want to add their profiles to the site).

Hopefully the above topics and exercises have given you lots of inspiration for exploiting the web as an enormous resource for use with your students!

Conclusion

EFL/ESL and general interest websites are worth considering if:
- you want to make exercises using authentic texts;
- you want to use interactive language exercises with your students;
- you want to use topical, authentic material with your students;
- you want information to complement a topic from your course book;
- your students are interested in a particular subject such as a specific sport;
- your students have internet access in the classroom or institution, or at home.

Chapter 3

WebQuests

The term WebQuest was coined by Bernie Dodge, a professor at San Diego University, in a 1995 article (available on the <u>WebQuest Page</u>). He defined a WebQuest as:

> *An inquiry-oriented activity in which most or all of the information used by learners is drawn from the Web. WebQuests are designed to use learners' time well, to focus on using information rather than looking for it, and to support learners' thinking at the levels of analysis, synthesis, and evaluation.*

At first sight this definition looks somewhat bewildering, so let's try to explain it in simpler terms. Basically a WebQuest involves giving your students a task. To complete the task, the students have to use resources on the internet (although not all the resources need to be online). They have to gather information, transform it in some way, and then produce some kind of output. The diagram below represents this process visually.

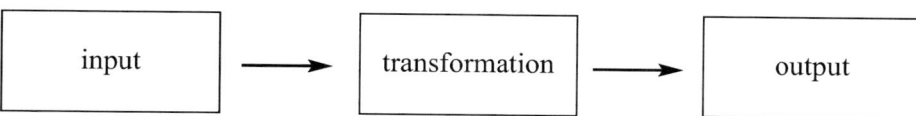

The three-part WebQuest model.

For example, a WebQuest might require a group of students to compare and contrast different viewpoints on a particular political issue, and then produce a presentation giving the students' views. WebQuests are superficially similar to 'Treasure Hunts' (activities where students are given a list of questions and have to find the answers using the internet) but there is one important difference - a WebQuest requires students to transform the information they obtain in some way, whereas a Treasure Hunt involves simply retrieving information. The reason why the WebQuest model places emphasis on transforming information is that it is based on constructivist learning theory. Constructivism lies somewhat outside the scope of this book, but suffice to say that it requires students to actively engage with the source material and use it to construct meaning, rather than just regurgitating the original material - hence the importance of transformation.

At this point we should perhaps mention that WebQuests were not originally designed for language learning. Rather, they were intended for use by elementary and high school teachers teaching subjects like Geography or Maths (generally within a North American context). However, many language teachers are interested in the possibilities of using WebQuests in language teaching. There is indeed a strong case to be made for using WebQuests in language learning, as they are arguably task-based, encourage learner independence, get the student engaged with authentic materials and are generally motivating and fun.

So what is a WebQuest, exactly? WebQuests which follow the original model developed by Bernie Dodge and his colleagues generally consist of five parts. These are outlined on the next pages.

3

WebQuests

1 Introduction

This is where you set the scene for your WebQuest. The aim of the introduction is to arouse the students' curiosity and make them want to do the WebQuest. Naturally this is especially important with younger students, who may be lacking in intrinsic motivation. Here you should communicate the Big Question which your WebQuest is addressing; this could be for example "How can the Israeli-Palestinian conflict be resolved?" (when we said Big Question, we meant big!), "What can be done to lessen the effects of global warming?" or "Where should we locate our new power plant?". Notice that you haven't yet told the students what they actually have to do yet - that comes next, in the Task stage.

2 Task

In this stage, you tell students what the output of the WebQuest will be. This could be a presentation, a report, a summary, a web page, or basically anything which involves the students transforming the information in some way.

3 Process

Here you outline what the learners will go through in order to accomplish the task you have set them. This is also the stage where you tell the learners which resources they will use. Naturally this will include the addresses of the websites you have chosen. However, don't think that a WebQuest has to use only websites as resources - offline resources such as reference books, newspapers or even real people (such as a local person who is an expert on the subject) can also be used.

Many WebQuests divide the work up into different roles, so that students are forced to co-operate in order to complete the task, so students would work in groups, and each group member would have a different role within the group. If you decide to use this approach, try to choose roles which reflect real life roles, for example professions like journalist, scientist, politician etc. The task should only be doable if the students with different roles work together. Naturally the work should be more or less evenly balanced between the different roles, and each role should have a similar number of resources available to it.

At this point you may also want to include scaffolding. Scaffolding is a term often used in relation to WebQuests, and is, as the metaphor suggests, a temporary structure designed to provide help at specific points in the learning process. It can provide guidance on how to gather, analyse and organize the information, and it should help learners act more skilled than they really are. The long-term goal of scaffolding is for learners to internalise structures so they can work autonomously.

Within the WebQuest context, three kinds of scaffolding are identified:

> **Reception scaffolding** helps students learn from a given resource and retain what was learned.
>
> **Transformation scaffolding** helps students with transforming the information, for example comparing/contrasting, finding patterns, brainstorming, or decision-making.
>
> **Production scaffolding** helps students with the production aspects of the task by providing them with templates, models, writing guides etc.

Within a language learning context, an example of reception scaffolding could be giving students advice in using an online dictionary. One example of transformation scaffolding could be giving students a chart to complete with the pros and cons for the different options they are considering, while an example of production scaffolding could be a list of useful language for making a presentation in English. Naturally these are all skills which the student can use in other contexts as well.

4 Evaluation

This is where the students are told how their performance will be evaluated. Here you should specify if the evaluation will be for the individual, the group, or both - the latter option will often produce the best results. Many WebQuest writers use a matrix to show how the work will be evaluated. The matrix below is taken from the Ellis Island WebQuest developed by Claude Covo-Farchi, Solange Soinard, Florence Viquerat and Philip Benz.

Criteria:	0 points	2 points	4 points	Your score:
Idea phase: before going on the internet	No preparation work.	Quickly noted a few ideas before going to the internet.	Carefully completed all questions in the introduction and task sections before going on the internet.	
Vocabulary phase	No vocabulary work.	Used vocabulary exercises and noted some words for later use.	Completed all vocabulary exercises and noted all new or important words or expressions. Used many of these words in later work.	
Online phase	Just clicked and watched.	Worked through the website step by step. Noted a few words or places for later use.	Both partners participated fully and effectively. Your notes include summaries or explanations in your own words.	
Diary preparation phase	Little real preparation.	Made a few notes for each section of the Diary Template.	Carefully prepared each section of the Diary Template and wrote out a first draft before checking grammar and vocabulary for the final composition.	
Final writing phase	Careless final work: your composition looks like a few lines of notes more than a carefully prepared composition.	Average final work: your composition is interesting, but there are problems with grammar, vocabulary or the logical development of ideas.	Excellent final work: your composition shows that you have worked on every step of the project, and carefully checked your grammar and vocabulary before handing it in to your teacher.	

5 Conclusion

Finally, the conclusion should bring closure and encourage reflection. If you can refer back to your introduction, so much the better. It should also summarise what has been accomplished and learned, and should encourage students to extend their thinking beyond the lesson by including rhetorical questions or extra links.

Finally, if you are planning to publish your WebQuest on the web or elsewhere, you should include a teacher's page explaining how to work with the WebQuest.

Using WebQuests

Having read the above description, you are hopefully keen to try out a WebQuest for yourself, and may be wondering where you can find them on the web. The best place to start is Bernie Dodge's excellent WebQuest site - it includes a table listing many of the WebQuests currently available, sub-divided by subject category.

As we mentioned before, WebQuests were not originally designed for language learning, so at the time of writing you won't find many WebQuests online which are specifically intended for language learners. However, many of those developed to teach other subjects are also usable with language students, especially if you have students who enjoy discussing controversial issues. The elementary and high school focus of the original WebQuest concept means that most of the WebQuests currently available are most suitable for children and teenagers. This doesn't mean, however, that WebQuests are not usable with adult learners. Some of the WebQuests written for teenagers can also be used with adults, and you can also argue that traditional Business English simulations are eminently suitable for adapting into WebQuests.

It is also possible to adapt an existing WebQuest to suit your own needs. You can save a web page to your hard drive by selecting, for example, *File > Save As* in your web browser. You can then open the page in a text editor such as Notepad and edit the content. If you don't feel comfortable working with HTML, you can also select the text from the original web page and copy and paste it into a word processor. You can then edit the text in the word processor and give it to your students as a printed worksheet.

Having looked at the WebQuests already available, you may decide that you want to write your own WebQuest, but you are worried that you don't know how to write web pages. Never fear. A WebQuest doesn't need to be a web page (although many are); it could just as well be given to students on a piece of paper - the format of the WebQuest is not important. The point of a WebQuest is that some of the information the students need to find is on the web, the instructions themselves do not need to be online.

But what if you do decide to write your WebQuest as a web page but are not sure your web design skills are up to it? One option would be to take a look at Chapter 8 on writing HTML. Another possibility is to use a template. Templates are available at Bernie Dodge's WebQuest website. With a template, the tricky technical stuff has already been done for you - you simply have to edit the HTML pages by opening them in a text-editing program (which could be Microsoft Notepad or even Word) and replace the dummy content with your own content.

Naturally, WebQuests also have their drawbacks. The most obvious potential problem is access to technology (which naturally applies to all the other media described in this book). However, in contrast to some of the other media, WebQuests are more amenable to being used in situations where students have limited access to computers. It is conceivable that you could do an entire WebQuest on paper, with the WebQuest itself being set as a worksheet, and the online resources printed out. Naturally one loses the interactivity that comes with accessing real websites, but the WebQuest is still do-able.

Another problem is 'link rot', which as the name suggest describes the phenomenon where links gradually become outdated. You can see this with several of the WebQuests already online, which have not been updated within the last couple of years - many of the links no longer work. Naturally it is essential to check all the links on a published WebQuest before using it with your students. If you find a link is broken, don't panic. Often the target page which was once linked to still exists, but its address has simply changed. In this case, it is sometimes possible to find the page in its new location by using a search engine - search for the title of the page, or the author. Alternatively, it is often possible to replace a page which has disappeared with another page with similar content. Of course, if you have written your own WebQuest, it is essential that you keep the links up-to-date. Bear the problem of link rot in mind when you are designing your WebQuest; you may want to avoid having the WebQuest dependent on a few very specific pages which may later disappear.

Another potential problem with WebQuests, which is simultaneously one of the great things about them, is that students have to engage with authentic materials. This means that it is challenging to design a WebQuest for low-level students. There are very few WebQuests already online which are suitable for use with low-level learners, as most published WebQuests are designed for native speakers of English. However, with a judicious choice of materials, and appropriate support in the form of scaffolding (see above), you could design a WebQuest usable with elementary or pre-intermediate students.

Another factor which one should be aware of when using WebQuests, is that as they are essentially based on completing tasks, there is generally very little focus on form. This may or may not be a problem, depending on your methodological approach, but you may feel that some focus on language is desirable. In this case you could for example pre-teach key vocabulary which will come up in the WebQuest, encourage students to make a note of new vocabulary and grammar they encounter while doing the WebQuest, and discuss language which came up during the WebQuest after the task has been completed.

As we mentioned before, WebQuests were not originally designed for language learning, and there is still a lot of work to be done on adapting the WebQuest model to best suit the needs of language learners. If you find yourself interested in WebQuests, you might like to collaborate with others in the active WebQuest community and help with the next stage in the evolution of the model. A good place to start is the WebQuest email discussion list – details of how to join are on Bernie Dodge's WebQuest page.

Conclusion

WebQuests are especially suitable for use with:
- younger learners;
- groups of learners;
- learners who enjoy discussing controversial themes;
- learners who enjoy collecting and analysing information;
- learners who can cope with authentic material on the internet;
- business English learners who wish to do simulations.

Chapter 4

CD-ROMs

CD-ROMs as a technology are not particularly new, having been around since the 1980s. They are a storage medium, similar to audio CDs, which can be used to store relatively large amounts of data, and offer teachers the possibility to incorporate multimedia into their teaching. CD-ROMs are extremely versatile and allow the learner to, for example, listen to audio, watch video clips, read texts and do interactive exercises. There are now many CD-ROMs on the market aimed specifically at language learners, from both large and small publishers. In addition, CD-ROMs produced for other markets, for example encyclopaedias, can also be used for language teaching. You can find a list of recommended language learning CD-ROMs in Appendix 2.

One name that often comes up when CD-ROMs and EFL are being discussed is Pete Sharma, to whom we owe many of the ideas in this chapter. His book *CD-ROM: A Teacher's Handbook* is an excellent resource if you want to find out more about using CD-ROM.

4
CD-ROMs

CD-ROM vs. internet

Before we look at what CD-ROMs can offer, let's consider briefly the relationship between CD-ROMs and the internet. The distinction between CD-ROMs and web-based materials is already blurring, with many CD-ROMs including links to online material. Some teachers might tend to think that CD-ROMs have now been superseded by internet-based resources. After all, on websites you can also do exercises and access multimedia elements such as audio and video. Why do we need to bother with CD-ROMs?

Two words: bandwidth and connectivity. Bandwidth refers to the amount of data which can be transferred over a particular data connection within a given amount of time. You can think of it as being equivalent to speed, with a faster connection having more bandwidth. Certainly you can watch video over the internet, but if you have a slow connection like a modem, the image is going to be the size of a postage stamp and poor quality to boot. The advantage of CD-ROM is that the information can be read much faster off the disk than it could be downloaded from the internet with a slow connection. So one point in favour of CD-ROMs is that they deliver better-quality audio and video.

The second term, connectivity, refers to how extensively a country or region is 'connected', i.e. how many people or households have any sort of internet access at all. In large parts of the world, such as Africa and China, internet access is still extremely limited due to reasons of infrastructure, finance or governmental policy. In such areas, CD-ROMs are likely to be much more useful (so long as learners have access to a computer) than websites.

Apart from these technical considerations, there are others advantages to using CD-ROMs. One is the simple fact that CD-ROMs are almost exclusively produced by publishers, whereas anyone can produce a website. The higher demands of making a CD-ROM mean that the quality is often (albeit not always) higher than that of home-made websites. For one thing, a published CD-ROM has almost certainly been checked by a professional editor – not something that can be said for all language learning websites.

Another factor is that CD-ROMs are not subject to the same technical restraints which apply to websites. Websites are generally written in HTML, which was originally designed purely to display text and is accordingly very limited. Although there are ways around its limitations, website designers are much more restricted than CD-ROM designers in terms of what they can achieve with design and interactivity.

A further aspect is that of control, which is particularly relevant if you are teaching younger learners. Asking students to access the web can require a constantly vigilant eye, in order to make sure they don't view inappropriate content. Working with CD-ROMs, on the other hand, is more predictable in that you know what content they will be accessing.

However, the above factors are likely to change in importance as the internet and access to it evolve. As broadband connections spread, more people will have access to high-quality video, and data transfer rates will cease to be an issue.

The range of high-quality language learning websites will undoubtedly continue to increase, probably in parallel with the increasing commercialisation of the internet. To put it crudely: you get what you pay for. As more people become prepared to pay for online content, more money will be invested in developing good-quality online materials.

Higher bandwidth will also decrease the limitations of current websites. Many more things are possible using, for example, Flash, than straight HTML. The fact that Flash files can be prohibitively large and therefore slow to download will become less important as connection speeds increase. However, multimedia CD-ROMs are likely to be around for a good few years yet.

Or rather, DVDs will be. DVDs have a significantly higher storage capacity than CD-ROMs and are likely to replace them as the medium of choice for multimedia. In this chapter, although we will be referring to CD-ROMs, most of these points will also apply to multimedia DVDs.

Practical considerations

If you are thinking of incorporating CD-ROMs in your teaching, it is worth spending some time thinking about the actual logistics. Will you use the CD-

4

CD-ROMs

ROM during class time, or for self-study? Will the student use the CD-ROM in the same place as the face-to-face teaching is taking place, or at home? Will the CD-ROM remain the property of the teacher or school, or will it be given to the student after the course?

Many schools have self-access centres, and CD-ROMs lend themselves very well to being used in such centres, being ideally suited to self-study. Some thought should be given to how to incorporate CD-ROMs into a self-access centre, as well as to how the self-access centre itself is set up. The following are some aspects you will want to take into account:

- How will the computers be arranged in the room? Many computer rooms have the computers arranged simply in rows, but this is not necessarily the ideal layout. Try to find a layout which maximises the possibility for students to interact. Is there a printer available so that students can print out materials from the CD-ROMs? Remember how important it is that students take away a hard copy of work they have done.

- Where will the CD-ROMs be kept, and who will be responsible for them? Will you have a booking system for using the CD-ROMs? Is theft likely to be an issue? Even if it's not, CD-ROMs can easily go missing, so how can you keep track of them? Some kind of sign-out sheet is a good idea. You may also decide to have the CD-ROMs themselves kept in a secure location, with only the cases on display, and have one person responsible for lending out the disks.

- Will students have a log to complete as a record of what they have done with the CD-ROMs? A learner log is especially important when students are using CD-ROM for self-study, as it allows them to keep a record of what they have done, and to make a note of their comments or queries. The log can also be used by teachers to set work for the students and keep track of their progress.

- Which CD-ROMs are likely to be most useful for your learners? Think about what age range you are dealing with.

Do learners need General English or Business English? Do your learners have any specific problems (such as pronunciation) which could be targeted with an appropriate CD-ROM? One good idea is to prepare a handout or booklet describing the various CD-ROMs, what level/age-group each one is most appropriate for and what language areas they are most useful for.

- Will you provide training for the students, to show them how to use the CD-ROMs? Without some kind of introductory session to introduce students to CD-ROM, the CD-ROMs are likely to remain unused. If you are in charge of other teachers, you may find the teachers also require training to convince them of the merits of using CD-ROM. You might also need to teach sessions on basic computer literacy such as starting Windows or how to use a mouse.

Incorporating CD-ROMs into a course

CD-ROMs are an ideal way to complement face-to-face teaching; on the whole they are not designed to replace it. There are various ways in which you can integrate CD-ROMs into a taught course.

- If you are teaching an intensive course you may want to schedule a period of self-study every day, which could include using CD-ROMs in a self-access centre. Remember to give students a log sheet so you can keep track of their work.

- On an extensive course, CD-ROMs could be used to set homework for students to complete between classes. The homework could be completed in the institution's self-access centre, or you could give students CD-ROMs to take home. (Whether this latter option is practical depends naturally on what kind of students you teach, and how trustworthy and reliable you consider them to be.) Alternatively, you could schedule a CD-ROM session during class time every few weeks.

CD-ROMs

- Within a Business English context, many teachers work in-company, with good access to technology. This makes using CD-ROM very straightforward (although you may want to check with the person responsible for the company IT facilities before installing new software on a particular machine). Allowing in-company students to borrow the CD-ROM between classes gives them an excellent way of practising in their own time; as the CD-ROM is installed on their own computer, they can easily spend a few minutes now and again working with the material.

- As an alternative to having students use CD-ROMs in your institution, you could also give students a CD-ROM to take away after a course, so that they continue to study. From a business point of view, this could be offered as an 'added value' component, which will likely be perceived by students as being worth more than a simple list of web links. You could even produce an individualised CD-ROM for each of your students just before they leave, containing various materials they have used or created; with CD burners becoming more and more affordable, this can make your school look particularly innovative at a very low cost.

Using CD-ROMs

So how does one actually use a CD-ROM? Generally speaking, when you use a CD-ROM for the first time, you will need to transfer certain files to the hard drive of your computer. This usually takes place with a minimum of effort on the part of the user – normally CD-ROMs are designed to carry out the installation almost automatically. Refer to the instructions on a particular CD-ROM to find out what to do. Often all that is required is to view the contents of the CD-ROM using (for example) Windows Explorer, and then click on the file called setup.exe. (If there is a file called readme.txt, it's generally a good idea to read this before you start!)

Once the CD-ROM has installed the necessary files on your computer, you will probably find there is a new icon on your desktop, or possibly in your programs menu. When you want to use the CD-ROM you simply click on this icon to start it, assuming of course that the CD-ROM itself is in your CD-ROM drive (unless you have copied all the files to your hard drive, in which case you don't need to use the disk any more).

So what do CD-ROMs actually provide? Language learning CD-ROMs generally offer a wide range of activities. These can include grammar and vocabulary activities, such as multiple choice, gap-fills or matching exercises.

Many CD-ROMs feature listening practice using audio and/or video. In fact, CD-ROMs are ideally suited to listening practice. One reason for this is that the student has the advantage that they can listen as often as they like. In addition, a tapescript and/or subtitles are usually also available. One advantage of using CD-ROM over traditional video is that students have more control, and can choose whether to watch the video with subtitles or not, and also have access to support, such as a dictionary, within the same program. Many non-language-learning CD-ROMs feature audio and video, which are also usable in teaching. However, make sure you check the level of the text before you try to use it in class – often material designed for native speakers is at too high a level for most learners.

CD-ROMs offer limited opportunities for speaking practice. Some CD-ROMs offer learners the possibility to record their own speech, then compare it to an original, then re-record themselves, as often as they wish. This approach may help certain students to improve their pronunciation, though others find it frustrating when they can't make their speech match the original completely; many teachers would argue that it's not necessary for a student to mimic a native-speaker exactly anyway. A variation on this is CD-ROMs with voice recognition facilities which give learners the possibility to take one role in a dialogue.

Reading is naturally also possible with CD-ROMs. Some CD-ROMs have exercises requiring students to read texts and answer questions. CD-ROMs produced for purposes other than language learning often have extensive reading texts which are also usable.

Writing, on the other hand, is a skill hard to address with CD-ROMs as it is

CD-ROMs

too creative for a computer to be able to assess (for the time being, at least). Many CD-ROMs aimed at language-learners do have gap-fill exercises, though, which can go some way towards written practice.

Ideas for using CD-ROMs in the classroom

Here are some ideas for using CD-ROMs (both those designed for language learning and those designed for other purposes) in the classroom.

- Dictionary CD-ROMs such as the Longman Interactive English Dictionary naturally lend themselves to a wide range of possible activities. These could include using the pronunciation facility to help students distinguish between minimal pairs or to categorise words according to word stress. Dictionary CD-ROMs often include picture libraries or diagrams – these make an excellent resource for teaching lexical sets like parts of the body or household objects. You could give students a printed diagram or picture and get them to label it using the picture on the CD-ROM. Often dictionary CD-ROMs include collocations and fixed phrases for words and can be used as a resource for lexical work, such as finding collocations for particular words.
- Encyclopaedias such as Microsoft's *Encarta* can be used as a resource for student presentations. Set students a topic to research (or let them choose their own) and give them a certain amount of time to prepare a presentation on the topic, using Encarta as a source of information. Some encyclopaedia CD-ROMs allow you to produce graphs of, for example, economic or demographic trends in a country. These can be used as visuals for student presentations, to help them practise language for talking about trends. Or get students to compare different countries, in order to practise comparatives.
- Some companies produce their own CD-ROMs with information for their employees, or with promotional material. Such company-specific material can be used as

authentic material with in-company students. If the CD-ROM is a reference guide for employees, this can provide raw material for a business simulation.
- Many business English CD-ROMs contain videos of actors acting out situations such as visiting a company or checking into a hotel. These can be used as input for role-plays – students can either watch the clip and recreate the situation as a role-play, or do the role-play first and then watch the clip to see how native speakers perform the same task.
- CD-ROMs can be used as a starting-point for pairwork. For example, you can introduce the general topic of the content of a CD-ROM. Half of the students now prepare some questions about the content while the other half explores the content of the CD-ROM and then tries to answer the questions which the first half have written for them. This can work particularly well with encyclopaedia CD-ROMs for example, which contain factual information about countries, sports, and so on.

Conclusion

CD-ROMs are suitable if:
- you have access to multimedia computers;
- you have no internet connection, or a slow connection, or if you do not want to use the internet as a resource for whatever reason;
- you wish to use good-quality audio and/or video;
- you wish to include self-study as a component of a course;
- students need extra practice in a particular area such as pronunciation or grammar;
- you would like to be able to control what the student can access;
- you wish to give students a 'bonus' to take away after a course.

Chapter 5

Text-chat, Internet Relay Chat and Instant Messaging

As the name suggests, text chat software allows you to chat using text. It was one of the first means of online communication to be invented, and as such it remains one of the more straightforward ways to 'talk' to people online, either on a one-to-one basis or in a group. If you've never used text chat, you can imagine it as being like a telephone conversation where, instead of speaking, you have to write down everything you say.

There are three main ways in which people text chat. We'll look at each in turn.

1. Chat rooms
2. Internet Relay Chat (IRC)
3. Instant messaging

Chat rooms

The first possibility usually involves you and your chat partner (or partners) logging on to the same chat room. This could be a public website and therefore open to anyone, or it could be restricted to certain users, for example the delegates at an online virtual conference. It could also be part of a learning platform (see Chapter 7 on Learning Management Systems for more information on this technology).

Normally when you log on to the chat website for the first time you have to define your user name, which doesn't necessarily have to resemble your real name. (With certain chat sites, you definitely wouldn't want to use your real name.) If you don't give a name, the program may automatically assign you a user name such as 'guest329', whereby the number after 'guest' is added sequentially, indicating the number of other guests logged in.

The website features a chat window and an input box, and often a list of the people who are currently in the chat room. You type your utterance into the input box and press return (or click on the appropriate button). Your message then appears in the chat window, next to your user name, so that people can

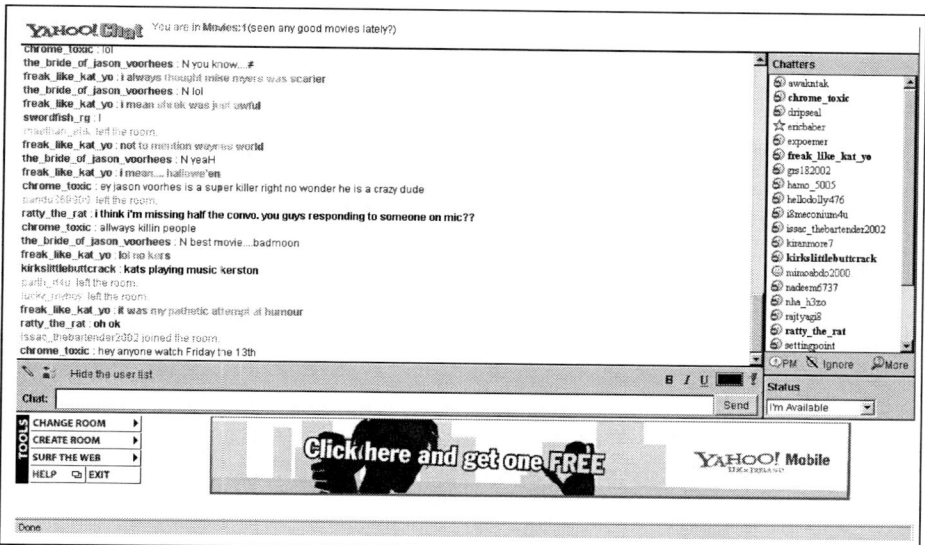

Yahoo! Chat room service

5

Text-chat, Internet Relay Chat and Instant Messaging

tell that you are responsible for this particular utterance. The other people in the chat room do the same thing, so that you see a sequence of utterances appearing on the screen, with the alias (the user name) of the person next to their comment. Sometimes the time at which the utterance was made is also shown. Each time somebody says something new, the conversation scrolls up a bit to make room for the new utterance, which is shown at the bottom. If there are several people in the chat room, the conversation may scroll so fast that it is difficult to keep track of what is going on. Being a fast typist is definitely an advantage in a chat room, and participating in text chat is a great way to improve your typing speed!

Naturally if there are more than a couple of people in the chat room, parallel conversations can develop and it can all get a bit difficult to follow (not unlike similar situations in the real world!). Some chat rooms allow you to whisper to another person so that only they can read your message. It's a good idea to learn how to 'whisper' very quickly. Inadvertently addressing all the chat parties in reply to a whispered comment is a common faux pas among chat novices, leading to at best non-sequitors and at worst deeply embarrassing situations. Another option in many chat rooms is to invite someone to go to another 'room' for a private conversation.

Chat rooms sometimes have a bit of a bad reputation. Admittedly many revolve around sex or tedious banter, but there are some which are more serious. For example, Yahoo! Chat has chat rooms dedicated to topics such as religion, education, or politics.

From the perspective of the language learner, chat rooms provide a useful opportunity for exposure to native speakers spontaneously interacting, with the added advantage that there is no equivalent to a mumble in text chat – misspellings aside, normally it's clear what people are saying. Also the chat can usually be copied and pasted, or saved, for the learner's future reference.

Whether a normal chat room can be used successfully for teaching is another question. With an open chat room, it's probably all a bit too chaotic and uncontrollable. One notable exception is the admirable Webheads project from Vance Stevens et al, where learners and native speakers meet once a week in a chatroom for conversation practice.

Internet Relay Chat

The second possibility is called Internet Relay Chat or IRC for short. (Confusingly, IRC has also become a generic name for any kind of text chat.) This requires a bit more effort. First of all, you have to download a piece of software called a chat client such as mIRC. Once installed, this software allows you to connect to the IRC network via an IRC server. You then choose a nickname which will be your virtual identity on IRC.

Next you have to choose a channel to join – think of a channel as a group of people having a conversation about a particular topic. There can be hundreds or even thousands of different channels on an IRC server, some of which are more or less permanent, while others are more temporary. Once you've joined a channel, you can start typing messages for other people who have also joined that channel to see. As in a chat room, it's possible to have a private conversation with someone. This, like other IRC operations, is accomplished with the help of a text command. (The use of text commands is one reason why IRC is harder to use than a website-based chat room.)

Our personal feeling is that IRC has to some extent been superseded by website chat rooms which don't require any additional software (apart from a relatively up-to-date browser), and don't require the user to remember commands. Certainly if you're an internet newbie then chat rooms are easier to start with.

Instant messaging

The third option is to use instant messaging (IM for short) software. IM has become increasingly popular in the last few years. An IM program basically consists of a window on your screen which shows your 'buddy list'. Your buddy list includes the people that you have invited to become your messaging partners ('buddies'), or who have invited you to be their buddy. These tend to be people you already know, but often complete strangers will ask if they can add you to their buddy list (naturally you don't need to agree). Think of a buddy list as something akin to your personal address book.

5

Text-chat, Internet Relay Chat and Instant Messaging

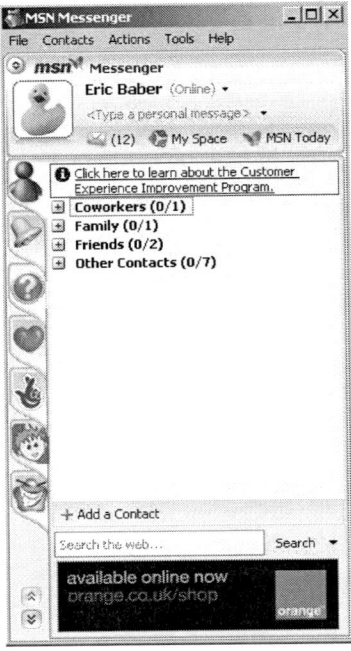

MSN Messenger instant messaging software showing groups of 'buddies'

Your buddy list shows which of your buddies are online, for example by way of an icon next to their name which changes colour depending if the person is on- or offline. If someone is online you can start a conversation with them, generally by simply clicking on their name. This sends them an invitation to start a chat. If they accept the invitation, a text chat window opens and you can write messages to each other. Some messaging programs allow you to use audio as well, so you can speak to your partner, just like on the telephone. Sometimes video is also available, if you have a webcam connected to your computer.

Usually you can chat with more than one person at a time – this is known as multi-way instant messaging. If there are more than two people in the chat, you can usually choose to 'whisper' to one person so that only they can 'hear' you, as with chat rooms or IRC.

However, it's definitely easier to use instant messaging with one person at a time, at least to start with.

Many IM softwares now have an option where you can use the service from a website, if you are using a different computer which does not have the software installed. At the time of writing, the latest development was instant messaging to mobile phones. IM services are evolving rapidly so more features will probably have been added by the time you read this.

With most instant messaging programs you also have a file transfer option which allows you to send files to each other, should you want to send, for example, a picture or a Word document to your buddy. (However you should be very wary of accepting files from strangers who you might meet online – they could contain viruses.)

Be aware however, that if you or your contact are behind a 'firewall' (a computer- or network protection mechanism, often used by companies but also individuals to protect their computers from hackers and viruses), then you may not be able to use all the features of instant messaging – audio, for example, can be a problem.

Some well known examples of instant messaging softwares include <u>AOL Instant Messenger</u>, <u>Yahoo! Messenger</u>, <u>ICQ</u>, and <u>MSN Messenger</u>. There are also some open-source versions available, such as Jabber and Trillian. Trillian has the advantage that you can use it to communicate with people who are using any of the major IM softwares. One disadvantage of the other softwares such as MSN Messenger is that the party you want to chat to must have the same IM software as you. However there is pressure from business and elsewhere for the different companies to make their IM systems compatible, which may be the case by the time you read this.

> **Jargon Box**
> Open source software or free software is software whose source code is available, unlike most commercial software. This allows users to change and develop the program, should they wish. Much (though not all) open source software is non-commercial.

The great advantage of using instant messaging over chat rooms or IRC is that chats are always private. (Well, almost private. Instant messaging is not particularly difficult for a malicious hacker to eavesdrop on – don't send anything sensitive such as a credit card number or a password by instant messaging – but an average user wouldn't be able to join a private instant-message conversation.) For the rest of this chapter we'll assume that you're using instant messaging for your teaching. Naturally the same techniques will apply if you choose to use chat rooms or IRC.

Teaching with text chat

So how can you teach with text chat? The easiest way would be to use it with a current student. Maybe you have a student who has moved away from the place where you live and can no longer come to class, but would like to continue learning English with you. Or perhaps you have a student who lives on the other side of town and it takes you an hour to travel to their home.

5

Text-chat, Internet Relay Chat and Instant Messaging

One great advantage of using instant messaging to teach is that it makes 'micro lessons' of, say, 20 minutes a real possibility. It's not worth anyone's time to travel somewhere for a 20-minute lesson, but if you're both at home or in the office then there's no reason why you can't have short lessons. 'Little but often' is a good language learning principle, so why not put it into practice and teach someone online every day for a few minutes? Another option would be to combine face-to-face teaching with online teaching using instant messaging. Imagine you're doing an intensive Business English course with a manager, meeting for 6 hours every day. Instant messaging creates the possibility of doing a 10 minute revision session online every evening.

Maybe you live in the middle of the Highlands of Scotland and not only is there no language school within a four-hour drive, there is no-one within your vicinity who wants to learn English. Instant messaging gives you the possibility to teach English from the comfort of your own home. To find students, you could advertise your services from your personal website, or get your old colleagues to recommend you to some students. (Of course, when you start doing this on a global scale, time zones become a problem.) How you handle payments for such a service is another question – it tends to be very difficult for private individuals to be allowed to accept credit card payments. However there are third party companies who will handle credit card transactions on your behalf, for a fee, naturally. Another alternative is PayPal, which is a popular way for private individuals or businesses to send payments to each other online.

Another option would be to have a social chat time for your students. Tell your class of 15 teenagers (who are all probably familiar with instant messaging already – ICQ in particular seems to be squarely aimed at the teenage market) that you will be online at, say, 8pm every Wednesday. Anyone who wants to practise their English can join the chat at that time.

What to do in your text chat/audio class

What about the actual logistics of teaching someone using instant messaging? The first step would be to check that they have the same instant messaging software installed as you, otherwise you won't be able to talk to each other. (Unless the competing companies have agreed on a common standard by the time you read this.) Alternatively you could use Trillian or one of the other instant messaging software packages that allow you to communicate with people using different systems.

Then you need to arrange a time to meet online. This could be done in class, by telephone or by email. If you're living in different time zones, make sure you take the time difference into account.

At the arranged time, both or all of you go online, and sign into the instant messaging service. (Most IM software packages sign in automatically when you go online, unless you tell them specifically not to. You may find you prefer the latter option – it gets a bit annoying if the software signs you in every time you want to check your email.) When you see your student is online, simply start a conversation with them by clicking on their name.

Now that you're in a text chat, what do you do? Well, the first decision is really whether you want to use exclusively text chat, or use audio. Text chat is a lot simpler, so you might want to stay with that initially. Audio involves both of you having a headset with earphones and a microphone, a sound card, and everything set up correctly. If either of you is not particularly technology-savvy, this could cause problems. Normally a little bit of experimentation with settings will generally fix any problems, but it can be very tricky to get a student to set everything up correctly if you can only communicate with them by text chat – especially if they have a low level of English and you don't speak their language. It is also worth pointing out that although it's possible to use audio with a microphone and separate speakers, this is generally a bad idea, as the audio coming out of the speakers will feed back into the microphone, and your partner will hear an annoying echo of everything they say. Using a headset circumvents this problem as the audio goes straight into your ears and is not picked up by the microphone. Plus a headset leaves your hands free to type. It might make you feel a bit silly, but no one's going to see you!

As for activities, a lot of things are possible in text chat, with a bit of imagination. Naturally straightforward conversation is the easiest option. If your student does actually live in a different country, you should have plenty to 'talk' about. The same techniques you would use in a one-to-one class will apply to text chat too (assuming you're just teaching one person, which is

5

Text-chat, Internet Relay Chat and Instant Messaging

likely). One approach can be to simply ask lots of questions and let the person talk. In a way text chat is easier than real conversation, because the delay between each person's turn means that both parties have time to think about what they want to say, and edit their utterance before they send it to their conversation partner. The pace of text chat tends to be slower than an oral conversation, due to the fact that everything has to be typed, plus any 'lag' (delay) which is introduced by the network.

If you're teaching someone whom you also teach face-to-face, then text chat is an ideal opportunity to review language covered in your normal classes. You could also use this time to ask your student for feedback on the course – the fact that text chat is less personal than face-to-face contact could help students to be more honest in their feedback.

Many games will work in the text chat environment, such as:

- you or the student can define a word for the other to guess – ideal as a revision activity;
- 'Twenty Questions', the game in which one person has to guess the other's identity or profession or whatever, by asking questions to which the other can only answer "yes", "no" or "maybe";
- one person can name a category and the other has 60 seconds to come up with as many items that belong to that category as possible.

Basically, any game which is purely verbal will work in text chat.

If you are feeling more ambitious, there are plenty of more structured activities you can do. Role-plays are easy enough to do in text chat, with the advantage that the students gain from having more time to think about their utterances than they would do in a real conversation.

One nice feature of text chat is that you can have text already prepared before the class, written in Microsoft Notepad for example, which you can then copy and paste into the chat window (see Appendix 4 on hints on how to copy and paste more easily). Be aware though that there is normally a limit to the number of characters that can be entered into the chat window at one time. This means that you could have pre-prepared role-play cards, which you paste into the chat window; if you have more than one student you could give them their role cards using the 'whisper' function. You could also copy the URL of a particular web page into the chat window, at which point it may turn automatically into a hyperlink (depending on which chat-program you are using). The student then clicks on this link to open the web page in their browser. (Remember you can have several different software packages, running in different windows, on your machine at one time.) You could set the student questions which they have to answer by reading the page, look at a page with interactive exercises together, or even send the student off on a WebQuest (see Chapter 3 on WebQuests for more information). You'll probably find as you become more experienced in online teaching that you get very good at switching between different windows on your computer! (For a tip on how to jump from one open window to the next, see Appendix 4, 'Toggling between windows'.)

You can also send a student an exercise by email, perhaps as a Microsoft Word document, which you then do together during your text chat class. Alternatively you could cut and paste each example or question into the text chat window, e.g.:

David says: Okay, Alex, what's the missing preposition in this sentence?

"I met him … a party."

Alex says: I think it's "at".

David says: Absolutely correct! Well done.

Your student could give you a talk or presentation, especially if you are working with audio. Perhaps he or she could prepare the presentation beforehand and send it to you as e.g. a PowerPoint file. Then you could both look at the slides together while your student gives the talk.

One very useful feature of text chat is that you can generally save a conversation that you've had with someone. (Be aware that, depending on the law in your country of residence, you might have to ask their permission first, especially in a public chat room.) You could use these saved chats as a resource for future lessons. For example, you could use them for error correction, either in a face-to-face lesson or in a later text chat. You could also use them to show your student how his/her English has improved, by comparing chats from the beginning and end of the course.

Limitations of text chat

Is there anything which can go wrong with text chat? It often depends on which software you are using. It is not unknown for chat rooms or IRC to crash completely, and there is almost always a time lag between your writing something and your partner seeing it. Instant messaging software seems to be more robust, and generally has less of a time lag, as you are communicating directly with each other as opposed to via a central server. Remember that communication problems are not necessarily caused by the technology – sometimes the reason a person is apparently not responding is simply because they're thinking about the answer or are slow typists, they've gone to answer the door, or even gone to the bathroom and not warned you! In general, text chat causes fewer problems than audio or video conferencing (which we will come on to later), though it does offer a more limited range of functions.

Conclusion

So what do students make of learning with text chat? Naturally this depends. The technophobes will not want to touch text chat with a proverbial barge pole, although you might be able to win them over by demonstrating how simple it really is. Other students may enjoy it, especially if it works out cheaper for them than face-to-face lessons. Certain students may prefer the text chat medium as it gives them more time to think about what they want to say. Students who feel self-conscious about their pronunciation may find it liberating. You might be surprised by how much shy students come out of their shells, especially if you are using a medium where people adopt new identities, such as a chat room – the empowering effect of having a new identity has often been commented upon.

On the other hand, if you are only using text chat with no audio, you may encounter resistance from people who are adamant that they want to speak. Another problem you might have is that some instant messaging programs (particularly ICQ) look like they were designed for teenagers, with lots of cute little icons and emoticons. This is all very well if you are actually teaching teenagers, but your middle-aged bankers might be less impressed. However, this can be expected to change in the future as instant messaging becomes more widely used in business, and consequently adopts a more 'serious' face.

To conclude, we would say that text chat/instant messaging is worth using as a teaching tool if the following conditions are true for you:

- you want to teach one-to-one (or possibly very small groups);
- you and your student live too far apart to make travelling practical, or you want to give short lessons, or you or your student are not able or willing to travel;
- you are confident using the software;
- your student is reasonably computer-literate;
- both of you have reliable internet connections;
- both of you have headsets and sound cards, should you want to use audio;
- both of you have the same software or compatible software;
- you speak your student's language or your student speaks good enough English that you can discuss the technical aspects in English;
- (assuming you require payment) you have some kind of payment scheme in place.

Chapter 6

Using Internet Audio/video-conferencing

Introduction

Audio/video conferencing has been around for a long time, but it is only with the widespread adoption of the internet, and relatively fast and stable connections, that it has become a realistic prospect for normal people. Before we continue we should clarify that there are two main types of audio/video-conferencing systems:

>1. **Dedicated audio/video-conferencing**. To use dedicated audio/video-conferencing you need dedicated equipment (hence the name) which usually consists of a high-quality camera, stand-alone microphone(s), a TV-screen and a connection to an ISDN line. When holding a dedicated video-conference you establish a direct ISDN connection to the other participant; this may incur substantial costs depending on the location of the other participant.

>2. **Internet audio/video-conferencing**. This requires a PC or laptop with at least a headset or microphone, and an optional webcam. The only connection needed is the regular internet connection. Because

all data flows via the internet, no long-distance call charges are incurred – instead, only your regular internet connection costs (if any) apply. As well as an audio and video connection, internet conferencing software typically offers functions such as text chat, file transfer, a whiteboard and other collaboration tools.

While dedicated audio/video-conferencing generally yields much better quality audio and video, it is also substantially more expensive both in terms of the necessary equipment and ongoing costs and has therefore traditionally only been used in the corporate and academic sectors. For the purposes of this book we will be talking about internet audio/video-conferencing since it is easily affordable to anyone with a computer with internet connection.

Internet conferencing vs. instant messaging

If you have just read the previous chapter on text chat and instant messaging, various aspects of internet conferencing as described above may sound pretty familiar. So what's the difference? As it happens, the gap between audio/video conferencing and instant messaging is steadily narrowing, as instant messaging software adds audio and video features. At the time of writing, the main difference is that audio/video conferencing software still tends to have more features (such as a whiteboard) than instant messaging software, but this could change in the future as instant messaging develops.

There are many audio/video conferencing software packages available, but few are free. At the time of writing, one exception is PalTalk, which allows you to make one-to-one and group audio and video calls. PalTalk is free to use, but has on-screen advertising. More information is available at the PalTalk website.

Another commonly-used conferencing software is Microsoft NetMeeting, which generally comes pre-installed with Windows. Although some people might prefer not to rely on Microsoft products, NetMeeting does have the advantage of being well-established and readily available – other free conferencing softwares have come and gone, but NetMeeting is still

Using Internet Audio/video-conferencing

available and still free. Interestingly enough, NetMeeting is commonly used in business for conferencing, especially in the USA, as it is completely free (assuming you have Windows, of course) – you only pay for your internet connection. In the examples that follow we'll look at NetMeeting, but the principles are generally the same for other conferencing software packages.

If you have Windows 95 or later on your PC, you will probably have NetMeeting installed already. It will probably be located in the menu

>Start > Programs > NetMeeting

If NetMeeting is not already installed on your computer, you can download it from the <u>Microsoft NetMeeting</u> website *except* for WindowsXP. If you are using WindowsXP there is no downloadable version of NetMeeting; instead, you will have to install it from the original WindowsXP CD-ROM.

When you start the program you may feel slightly bewildered by all the different windows and icons on offer. The illustration below explains what the different parts are.

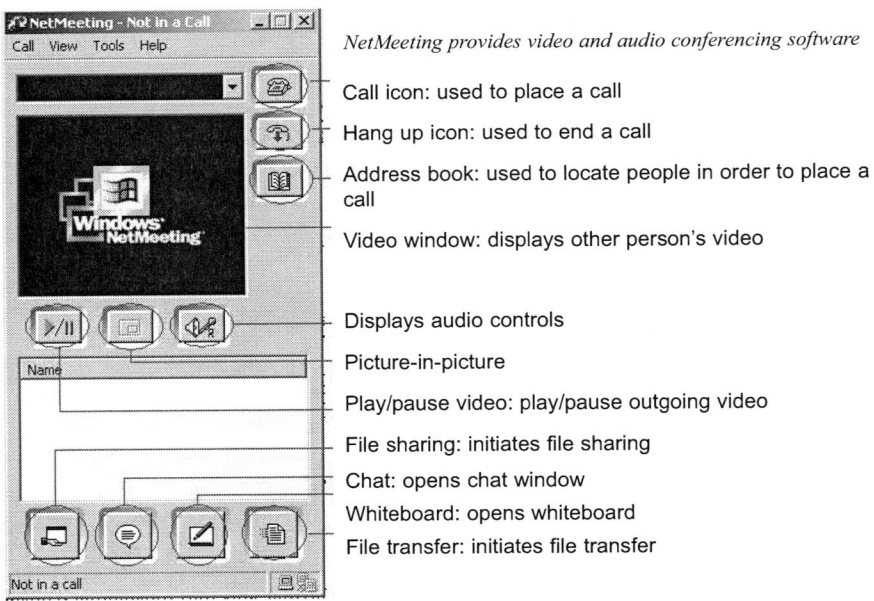

NetMeeting provides video and audio conferencing software

Call icon: used to place a call

Hang up icon: used to end a call

Address book: used to locate people in order to place a call

Video window: displays other person's video

Displays audio controls

Picture-in-picture

Play/pause video: play/pause outgoing video

File sharing: initiates file sharing

Chat: opens chat window

Whiteboard: opens whiteboard

File transfer: initiates file transfer

Starting a NetMeeting call

When using NetMeeting, you first of all have to establish a connection with your conversation partner. Naturally both you and your partner have to be online before you can set up a connection. There are various ways of establishing a call:

1. The easiest way to make a connection with NetMeeting is paradoxically by using another piece of software, MSN Messenger (see Chapter 5 on text chat for more information). Using MSN Messenger, you right-click on your partner's name in the buddy list (assuming that they are online) and then choose the option Start NetMeeting. NetMeeting will begin automatically on your computer and your partner will be notified that you are trying to start a NetMeeting call. If they accept, your NetMeeting call is established.

2. Another method is for both you and your partner to log on to the same online directory by selecting Call > Directory in NetMeeting (for a list of currently available NetMeeting directories (also called ILS – Internet Locator Service) visit the NetMeeting HQ website). You can then click on the name of your partner in the directory to start a call. A word of caution – these directories tend to be frequented by people with intentions that have little to do with language learning, and much to do with exploring the erotic possibilities of webcams. If you are logged on to a directory you may find random strangers inviting you to enter into conversation with them. If you do not want to speak to them, simply refuse the invitation – NetMeeting always asks for confirmation before beginning a call.

3. The third option is to call someone using their IP address. An IP address is a unique identifier that your computer receives when you log on to the internet, so that your computer can be identified. Some people have permanent IP addresses, but if you connect to the internet through a service provider you will probably receive a different IP address every time you go online. If you know your partner's IP address you can call them by entering the IP address into the box above the video window in NetMeeting. To find out which IP address you have once you are online, select the menu option Help > About Windows NetMeeting and it will tell you your current IP address. You can then email this address to your partner, and they can call you.

Once you are in a call you will see your name and your partner's name in the window below the video window. Assuming you both have headsets with microphones, you will be able to speak to each other. You may have to tinker with the audio settings for best results. Don't use a microphone and speakers as this will cause your partner to hear an echo, as a result of the output from the speakers feeding back into the microphone. If you and/or your partner have a webcam connected you will be able to see video as well (note that it is also possible for only one person to have a webcam, in which case the other person will be able to see the webcam user, but not vice-versa). With a slow connection such as a modem you may decide not to bother with video, as it requires more bandwidth than it is maybe worth. You may notice that the quality of the audio connection diminishes when video is also being transmitted, in which case you may want to switch off the video in order to improve the audio again.

You can also do text chat with your partner by clicking on the chat icon. This functions much like a normal chat program such as MSN Messenger – you type your remark into the input box and press send. It then appears in the dialogue window, as do your partner's remarks. You might be wondering why you would want to bother with text chat, when you can have audio and video as well. However the text chat function can be useful if you want to send, for example, a website or email address to your partner. Also if a third or fourth person joins the NetMeeting call (theoretically you can have as many people in the call as you want), only the first and second person will have an audio connection – the rest will have to rely on text chat. (There is a means to get multiway audio – i.e. audio for more than 2 people – using NetMeeting, but it requires extra equipment and is expensive and is therefore outside the scope of this book. If you are interested in learning more about this, though, the Meeting by Wire website is an excellent source of information.)

One of the most useful features of NetMeeting for teachers is however the whiteboard, which is designed to be analogous to a real whiteboard, allowing both parties to write and draw in a shared space. This is started by clicking on the whiteboard icon or selecting Tools > Whiteboard. The whiteboard opens and both parties see the same whiteboard window. (It may take a few seconds for the whiteboard to initialise, especially if you or your partner have a slow connection, and you may find that the audio quality is affected during this time. Relax and wait and everything will be okay.)

On the left side of the whiteboard are a selection of tools, which can be used to type on the board, draw lines, rectangles and ellipses, highlight text, and point at text using a moveable 'hand', among other functions. Once you have created elements (such as pieces of text or shapes) on the whiteboard you can move them around. This enables you to create, for example, a matching exercise where the student has to match words from two lists by moving them around, or an exercise where the student matches words and pictures.

The whiteboard can have multiple pages, which you switch between using the arrow keys in the bottom right hand corner. If you have multiple pages on your whiteboard, you may want to take advantage of the synchronisation function. When the whiteboard is 'synchronised', if one person scrolls around the whiteboard, or changes to another page, then the other person sees their whiteboard perform the same movement. If the whiteboard is unsynchronised then each person can move around their whiteboard (flip between pages, scroll on a page etc) without the other person being taken to the same 'location'. However any change to the actual elements on the whiteboard will still be registered on the other person's whiteboard. You may wish to employ the synchronisation function when teaching, so that you know what your student is up to – synchronising whiteboards means that s/he can't sneak off to another page without your knowledge.

One very handy feature of the whiteboard is that you can save whiteboards and open them again later, just like any other files. So you can prepare a whiteboard for a class in advance, save it to your hard drive, then open it once you have established a connection with your student. Although it is possible to include images on your whiteboard (by copying and pasting from another program, or by grabbing an image from the PC screen using the 'select area' function), you should keep these to a minimum, unless both you and your student have fast internet connections. Each image increases the size of your whiteboard, and the greater the file size, the longer it will take to open. Similarly, large whiteboards can sometimes lead to problems with the software or connection. (The graphics you create within the whiteboard itself, such as the rectangles and circles, do not greatly increase the file size.)

How to teach using internet audio/video-conferencing

So how can you actually use audio/video-conferencing software like NetMeeting for teaching? Unless you simply want to converse with your student, the secret is to make good use of the whiteboard. This will generally involve preparing a whiteboard for the class in advance. Most things you can do with a coursebook can also be done with the whiteboard – some examples are:

- cloze exercises;
- matching exercises;
- reading texts;
- discussion activities;
- ranking activities.

It's simply a question of typing the text on to the whiteboard, or cutting and pasting it from another document. The whiteboard has some advantages over a textbook, primarily that elements can be moved around, which makes matching or categorising exercises more interesting. Manipulating the elements on the whiteboard takes a little bit of practice, as you have to be careful to click exactly on the element that you want to move. This can sometimes be difficult if there are a lot of elements on the whiteboard.

The fact that your whiteboard can have multiple pages means that it is possible to prepare fairly sophisticated, well-structured, lessons. For example on the first page you could have a warm up activity, then on the second page a reading text, with a definitions game on the third page. It is also possible to have partner work where each partner looks at a different page of the whiteboard. Hence an online lesson can be created in much the same way as you might structure a traditional lesson in the classroom.

Another useful feature contained in NetMeeting is the file sharing facility. Using this function you can open any file you have stored on your computer and allow your student to see it, or even work on it. It also works the other way around – students can open files on their computer and you can view them. Some uses of this tool are as follows:

- Students can prepare homework between online lessons and then show you in the next lesson. You can then make corrections if need be, or talk about certain parts with the student and ask them to update certain passages immediately.
- A Business English student can go through PowerPoint presentations with you that they need to give in real life. This allows them to iron out any mistakes in the presentation and to gain confidence for the big day.
- If you have created exercises for classroom use in another program (such as Microsoft Word) you can reuse them in your online lesson.

A real benefit of file-sharing is that the other person does not need to have the relevant software package installed on their computer. If your student wants to share a PowerPoint presentation on their computer with you, for instance, you do not need to have PowerPoint installed on your computer since you are effectively sharing theirs.

A drawback of the file-sharing tool over the whiteboard is that in file-sharing only one person can edit a document at a time, unlike the whiteboard, where everyone can type, move objects and so on at the same time. If you're teaching a one-to-one lesson, though, the file-sharing function is likely to be very useful.

One thing that is slightly tricky to do during an audio/video-conferencing lesson is listening exercises. Let's say you have an audio connection to your student which is working fine, and you also have an audio file on your computer which you want to play down the line to your student. Intuitively you would think this would be very straightforward. Unfortunately, it's not. The reason why this is probably not going to work is the fact that the audio/video program is very likely monopolising the audio capability of your computer. The alternative is to break the audio link temporarily – reverting to text mode only – while the student goes to listen to a sound clip on a website. Alternatively you could send them the sound clip by email in advance, then tell them during class when you would like them to listen to it.

Integrating internet conferencing into your teaching

So why would you want to teach via audio/video-conferencing software? Like text chat software, it is useful if your student is not able to travel, if you or your student is geographically isolated, or you want to teach very short lessons. However audio/video-conferencing takes a bit of getting used to, so you probably wouldn't want to use it with a student who has little experience of using technology, at least not in the first class! Similarly, as the teacher you will probably want to practise using the software with a friend before trying to teach with it. One particular challenge of using audio/video-conferencing software is that if you are only meeting your student online, you will have to teach the student how to use the software while communicating with the student using the software itself. (Imagine using a telephone to explain to someone how to use a telephone.) For this reason, you might want to send your students instructions on how to use the software by email, if it is not possible to meet the student face to face to explain how to use it. This is one reason why you might not want to use audio/video-conferencing software with low-level students, unless you are able to explain the software in their own language.

Like other technologies, there are different modalities for incorporating audio/video conferencing in your teaching. For example, you might have a student who you have only ever met and taught online. It is probably easier to work with a student online if you have met them face-to-face, but it is certainly possible to establish a positive working relationship purely through online meetings. In this situation, you may want to use a webcam to let students take a look at you, at least in the first online meeting. It seems to be easier to communicate with someone when we have a visual image of them in our head.

Alternatively, you may want to supplement face-to-face teaching with online meetings. For example, imagine that you are teaching a one-to-one intensive course, where you meet the student for several hours face-to-face in a school. After class, you can have a fifteen minute online meeting once you are both home in the evening, in which you revise the material covered in the day's lesson. Or maybe you teach intensive courses at a school in the UK, where students come for one or two weeks. Audio/video-conferencing gives you the chance to offer the students extra lessons, before and/or after the course, when they are in their home country. This is a very attractive option for schools in English-speaking countries, as it allows them to sell additional teaching hours to their students. From the student's point of view, this modality is also attractive – they can build on what they have achieved during the intensive course, with the same teacher who they already know.

Also from a business point of view, one reason you might want to investigate using conferencing software is that this is one kind of e-learning that students are prepared to pay for. Few people are likely to want to pay to access your website with interactive exercises, no matter how attractive and pedagogically sound they are. There is simply too much free stuff available on the web already. But students are definitely willing to pay for live on-line teaching, as they feel that they are getting something tangible for their money (which indeed they are!).

If you are teaching students in companies or other large organisations, there is one snag associated with audio/video conferencing that you should be aware of. Generally speaking, company or institutional networks are protected by 'firewalls' which are designed to stop viruses or malicious hackers entering the system. Unfortunately firewalls often play havoc with audio/video conferencing software like NetMeeting. If you want to use NetMeeting within a firewall-protected environment, you may have to liaise closely with the person responsible for the network in order to get NetMeeting working successfully.

Conclusion

Despite the relatively steep learning curve and possible technical problems, it is well worth investigating the possibilities of using conferencing software. The potential it offers for teaching is great indeed.

To conclude, audio/video-conferencing software is most suitable for use if:

- either you or the student cannot travel to meet face to face, or do not want to travel;
- either you or the student are geographically isolated;
- both you and the student are relatively comfortable with using technology;
- the student is intermediate level or above, or you speak the student's mother tongue;
- both you and your student have headsets;
- both you and your student have relatively stable internet connections, the faster the better.

Chapter 7

Learning Management Systems

The previous chapters have covered various stand-alone technologies such as web-based exercises, discussion forums, text chat, and audio/video-conferencing, each with their own advantages and disadvantages. This chapter will look at systems that integrate some or all of these different technologies in a so-called 'learning management system'.

> **Jargon box**
> Learning management systems are also variously referred to as 'learning platforms', 'course management systems', or 'virtual learning environments'.

A learning management system (LMS) is basically a package which combines various e-learning technologies in order to gain the maximum benefit from them, and to provide integrated, cohesive, online courses. In brief, in learning management systems:

- teacher and student profiles can be created;
- content can be made available to students in a variety of formats – web-based (i.e. HTML), Acrobat (.pdf) files, Microsoft Word (.doc) and so on;
- instructors can design various types of exercises (multiple

7 Learning Management Systems

choice, gap-fill etc) which can be self-marking;
- teachers can assign exercises to specific students and keep track of their progress;
- students and teachers can communicate asynchronously by email or discussion boards, and synchronously via text or voice chat.

We will go into greater depths on each of those areas further below.

There are many learning management systems on the market which offer a similar variety of tools and functions. Most companies which advertise themselves as e-learning companies are actually offering learning management systems, with or without pre-built content. Many of these systems are high-end and aimed at corporate or institutional users, and generally require a substantial investment in time and money. As such, they are out of the reach of most ELT teachers, unless you are in charge of choosing an e-learning system for an organisation like a university or a company. If you are simply looking for a way to teach your private students one-to-one over the internet or to use the internet to supplement your classroom teaching, then a learning management system is probably overkill. Despite the high cost of many LMSs, there are some alternatives which are more accessible to the language learning market, which we will look at later.

If you are purchasing a learning management system, there are generally two models you can go for. The LMS company can give you access to the LMS running on their server, via the internet; this is known as the Application Service Provider (ASP) model. Alternatively, you can buy a license to install the LMS on your own server, which gives you more control of the LMS. This option is usually much more expensive, however, and also means that you have to have all the technical know-how needed to install the LMS software on your server and maintain it.

> **Jargon box**
> 'Blended learning' or 'blended solution' are two buzz phrases that often come up in connection with LMSs. They both refer to the practice of combining online courses (often delivered using an LMS) with face-to-face training. Many people consider blended learning to be more motivating and effective than e-learning alone.

What is a learning management system?

Most learning management systems have certain features in common. Naturally features and functionality vary from system to system, but the following description should give you some idea of what a learning management system is capable of.

Generally learning management systems have four main areas of functionality. These can be classified as content management, communication, assessment and control.

1 Content management

Learning systems generally have some kind of entry page (portal interface) which both students and teachers access each time they log on to the system. From this interface, users can access all the different features within the LMS. The interface provides users with basic course and personal information management tools. For example, users might see announcements about their course, check the calendar for upcoming events or submission deadlines, read what their current assignments are, and check their grades. They can access courses through links in the portal; the teacher can specify which students can access which courses. Users can also maintain their personal information using tools such as a personal calendar or address book.

Instructors meanwhile can use the portal interface to make learning materials available to students. They can create materials directly by using the interface or upload pre-existing files onto the course website. LMSs often support different file formats such as Microsoft Office or PDF; this allows material created for other uses to be incorporated into the online course. You do need to be aware of the fact, though, that not everything produced for offline courses will work well in the online or self-study environment – you may well need to adapt existing materials before uploading them into an LMS. The instructor can also specify when the content should be released – you might decide that a particular lesson should only be available after a certain date. You can also specify that a certain lesson must be completed, perhaps with a certain grade, before the next one can be begun.

2 Communication

Most LMSs provide both synchronous and asynchronous communication tools. For example, with many LMSs you can create discussion forums, and define their properties, such as who is allowed to contribute, and how the forum is displayed. Often it is possible to conduct live online text or voice chats, draw in a shared whiteboard, or work together in a virtual classroom environment. Usually a 'digital drop box' allows students to submit work and assignments. With some LMSs the teacher can create groups of students for collaborative work and enable protected discussion boards, virtual class rooms and file exchanges for each group.

3 Assessment

One very important feature of LMSs is assessment. This is naturally one clear advantage that LMSs have over (for example) e-learning websites. Learning management systems give instructors the possibility to create and administer quizzes and surveys. Normally you can use many different question types such as multiple choice, multiple correct, true/false, matching, ordering, fill in the blanks or essay. Apart from the essay question type, all other questions can be corrected automatically by the system, giving the learner instant feedback on their performance. Often you can include multimedia or other attachments with assessment questions. Tests can also be password-protected and/or timed. You can specify when assessments are released, and when they are recalled, so that students must take the test within a certain time period. Finally, you can create statistical reports of student answers, so you can see how well your students got on in the tests.

4 Control

Learning management systems allow instructors to monitor, control and customise their course websites, generally all from a web browser. It is normally easy to enrol and un-enrol individuals or groups of students. With some systems you can also choose advanced options such as limited-time self-enrolment or password-protected enrolment. You can recycle courses between academic terms by automatically resetting discussion boards, assessments etc. You can also track student progress, grades and course content usage.

In addition, many learning management systems also have extra components available for the system which allow you to extend its functionality. For example, you might be able to choose to incorporate an instant messenger, a dictionary or thesaurus, or a WYSIWYG web page editor into the system.

Another way in which you can customise most learning management systems is by changing the look of the interface. You can generally add your own logos, change the background colours, and change the appearance of navigation buttons and tabs. If you are working within an institution with its own brand image then this can be a very attractive option.

Factors involved in using LMSs

Probably the first decision you will have to make, once you have chosen to use an LMS, is whether the online training will be standalone, or be combined with face-to-face teaching (the so-called blended solution).

Naturally your decision will be influenced by factors such as the location of students and the feasibility of meeting face to face. If the course is entirely online, then you will have to think carefully about when online meetings (using text or voice chat) will take place – an issue which is even more complicated if participants live in different time zones. If students are only ever going to meet online, you will have to think about how to create a good group dynamic. Perhaps you may wish to schedule a "getting to know you" session at the start of, or even before, the course, to let participants get used to the idea of meeting online, and to break the ice with the other students.

Similarly, if you decide to incorporate online meetings into your blended solution, then careful consideration needs to be given to how often face-to-face and online meetings will take place, and at what times. It's probably a good idea to give students a choice of online meeting times, as you are unlikely to find one time which will suit everyone. You will also need to consider whether these meetings will be an optional extra, or an integral part of the course. Will you award grades for participation in the meetings? Will an instructor always be present?

One important consideration in using an LMS is how you will instruct students in the use of the system. Although LMSs are generally designed to be as user-friendly as possible, users still need a little time to get accustomed to working with them, especially as the concept of an LMS will be new to many people. Most LMSs have so many features that a novice user could feel overwhelmed without proper support. One option is to provide the students with a tutorial in using the LMS before the course begins. With a blended solution this is straightforward and would naturally form part of the first face-to-face meeting with students. If the course is entirely online then training the students becomes both more important and more problematic. You may wish to send the students a tutorial as a Word document, or provide a web page which teaches students how to use the system. Another alternative is to start off with a series of tasks you send students by e-mail, each task leading them to explore a further function of the LMS. One key question here is if the tutorial or tasks will be in English or in the students' own language. With lower level students, or with monolingual classes, the second option probably makes more sense.

Motivation is a key factor when using LMSs. Experience suggests that students often need external motivation to make the best out of self-study materials (which tend to be a major component of courses delivered with LMSs). Left to their own devices, students will probably not do as much work as you would like them to do, especially once the initial interest of doing something new has worn off. One way to increase student motivation is by giving them regular targets. For example, you might specify that certain exercises must be completed by a certain date. Setting regular tests is also a way to make sure students study in their own time. One enormous advantage of using a learning management system is that it is very easy for the teacher to keep track of what students have done. If you notice that one student has not been doing as much as she should have, then sometimes a simple email of encouragement will suffice to improve her performance. Meeting your students regularly face-to-face can also help to increase motivation. You could for example set homework in class to be completed online before the next meeting. With a little bit of friendly pressure you can provide the motivation that students need to ensure they complete the tasks you set in the intervening period. In our experience, students generally don't want to feel that they are letting their teacher down, and will make an effort to do the homework in time.

One major factor to think about when deciding whether or not to use a learning management system is content. Generally when one purchases a license for a learning management system, one receives access to the various tools and server space, but without receiving any actual course content. (Some learning management systems do have content – often produced by established publishers – which can be bought as modules. Bear in mind however that this content will not necessarily address the needs of your particular students.) You as the instructor (or your colleagues) will probably have to produce the content yourselves, using the authoring tools provided with the system, or by uploading content from other sources. Although producing materials with good authoring tools should be relatively straightforward, one should not underestimate the time it takes to write material, especially if starting from scratch. And remember that the success of the course will ultimately depend on the quality of the course materials.

Finally, if you are administering tests with a learning management system then you must consider the question of who is actually taking the test. Generally there is no way of checking if the person who is supposed to be taking the test is actually the person who really took it. Naturally students may feel the temptation to get a talented friend to take the test on their behalf. One way to deal with this is to weight the test marks so that no one test contributes so much to a student's final grade that they might be tempted to get someone else to do the test for them.

Examples of LMSs

So which learning management systems are realistically within the reach of ELT teachers? Three names which people often think of when learning management systems are being discussed are Blackboard, WebCT, and Virtual-U.

At the time of writing, Blackboard allows teachers to create a free 60-day trial course website. This gives you unlimited use of a course website for 60 days and 5MB of storage space for course materials. The course itself is hosted on the Blackboard servers, where you as the teacher and the students can access it anytime from the web. Alternatively you can pay US$295 and receive unlimited use of a course website for one year, with 25MB of space for course materials and technical support from the course instructor.

WebCT offers a similar deal. Unlike Blackboard, you purchase course space with WebCT through a reseller in your country, so prices can naturally vary. Just to give you an idea of prices, at the time of writing you could purchase a license for WebCT at the price of €250 for 12 months, plus a fee per user, which varies between €10-18 depending on the number of users.

At the time of writing, Virtual-U from Virtual Learning Environments Inc. only offers a single-server license, which means you have to install the software yourself on your own server. However this gives you an unlimited number of users. Currently this costs US$995.00, which is substantially cheaper than the own-server options from Blackboard and WebCT.

Naturally these prices and offers will change over time, so please refer to the companies' websites for more up-to-date information.

Conclusion

Learning management systems are a good choice if:
- you are teaching within an institution such as a university or company where there is a large budget available for an e-learning system, and a large number of students to take advantage of it;
- it is important to you to have a well-structured, professional-looking, and integrated online course;
- you wish to combine different technologies such as audio-conferencing, self-study material and discussion forums;
- you wish to teach groups of students online;
- you are willing and able to develop your own content.

Chapter 8

Creating Your Own Website

Reading the title of this chapter, you might ask yourself why you would want to bother creating your own website. After all, isn't it too much work, and best left to the professionals? Actually, you might be surprised how easy it is to produce a simple website. And there are many reasons why you might want to have your own web presence. Perhaps you have your own language school, or work as a freelancer, and want to promote your services.

A website is a way to get your name known and can even replace brochures as your main publicity material. Maybe you are thinking of teaching online using audio/video-conferencing and want to find students. Or you want to create your own website with English language exercises, either for your own students or for the entire online language learning community. Possibly you would like to create a website for a particular class that you are teaching, with useful links or homework assignments.

Having your own website can be an asset in so many different ways. And apart from anything else, they are a lot of fun to make. You might even decide (like a friend of ours did) to give up English teaching altogether and become a professional web designer!

8

Creating Your Own Website

What is HTML?

Once you've decided you want your own website, you have to create the actual content. As it happens, there are many ways to create a web page, many of which mean that you don't actually need to know anything technical such as HTML, the stuff that sites are made of. However, knowing a little bit about it helps, so we thought we'd start with a brief introduction of what HTML is.

The first thing you should know is that a web page is written in HTML, which stands for HyperText Markup Language. (Actually, these days many are written in XHTML, but let's not worry about that for the moment.) This lengthy name may appear rather intimidating at first glance, but don't let it put you off. As with many computer terms, it's a lot more straightforward than it first appears. Let's start with the word hypertext. The best example of hypertext is a web page. Web pages normally have text with links in it, with these links generally being underlined. You click on the link and you go somewhere else (either to another page or another paragraph within the same page) or you get a picture or whatever. So hypertext simply means text with links in it.

What about markup? You can think of markup as being similar to formatting. With a markup language you specify how a document is structured and how you want it to be displayed. Basically it's like saying "here's my document, it's got a title and three paragraphs and I want the headings displayed in bold". So HTML is simply a language which describes how a document is structured and displayed.

It's important to be aware that HTML is not a programming language. HTML is really just for formatting – if you want to do anything more fancy such as accepting input from the user and then doing something with this input, you're going to need another language such as JavaScript or PHP. We'll come onto those later on.

Creating a web page

So how do you actually create an HTML document, i.e. a web page? Probably the absolutely easiest way (though not the 'cleanest' – see below for what we mean by that) is with a word processor like Microsoft Word. If you want to try this, write a short text in Word. Then go to the File menu, select Save As, and choose 'web page' from the file type menu. Click on OK and Word will save your document as an HTML file. Remember where you saved it.

If you then find this file on your hard drive, you'll notice it has the extension .htm or .html. (The extension is the bit after the dot in the file name which tells you what type of file it is.) This means that the file is an HTML file. If you click on this file, Windows will automatically open it in your standard web browser (probably Internet Explorer), rather than in Word. Hey presto! You've just created your first web page. If you wanted to, you could publish this on the WWW and anyone else with a web browser would be able to look at it.

At this point, let us show you a nice little trick. Go to the View menu in your browser, and select the Source option (it might be worded slightly differently, depending on which browser you're using). Your browser will now show you the HTML code for the page (this is called the source code). This is a very useful technique for learning HTML – if you want to find out how to do something, simply find a web page which has done it already, then look at the source code and see how the author managed it. You can also copy this source code and use it in your own pages, instead of rewriting it from scratch.

If you're looking at the source code for the file you created in Word, it probably seems pretty intimidating. Don't worry – Word produces very complicated, cluttered HTML, which is one reason why it might not be the best way to produce your web pages. HTML can be a lot simpler than this.

Another way to produce web pages is by using an HTML editor such as Microsoft Front Page, Macromedia Dreamweaver or Adobe GoLive. If you're using Windows, you might already have Front Page or FrontPage Express on your computer. Many professional web designers use

Dreamweaver or GoLive, but they're not cheap. However there are also many free HTML editors you can download from the Internet, such as Amaya or 1st Page 2000 – see the Appendix for a list of links. These editors can make life a lot easier, and speed up the whole web page creation process. With many of them you don't even need to know any HTML – you simply work with your text almost as if you were using a word processor.

However, you'll be able to do much more with your web pages if you do know some HTML. And the good news is that HTML is really easy to learn – you can get the basics down in an afternoon. In the next section we're going to give you an introduction to HTML.

First steps with HTML

First you're going to need a text editor. If you're using Windows, we recommend you use Notepad – generations of web page designers have started off with it. You should be able to find it by going to Start, then Programs, then Accessories. It looks like a little blue notepad (surprisingly enough). Open it up, then type the following into it, exactly as it's shown below.

```
<HTML>
<HEAD>
<TITLE>My first web page</TITLE>
</HEAD>
<BODY>
Hello world!
</BODY>
</HTML>
```

Then go to the File menu, and select Save As. Type firstpage.html where it says File name. Make sure it says All Files (*.*) in the Save As Type field. Press return to save it to your hard drive, remembering where you saved it.

Now open up your browser, select Open from the File menu, and find your firstpage.html file (you might have to click on the Browse button to find it). Open the file and you will see your web page displayed in the browser. It should look something like this:

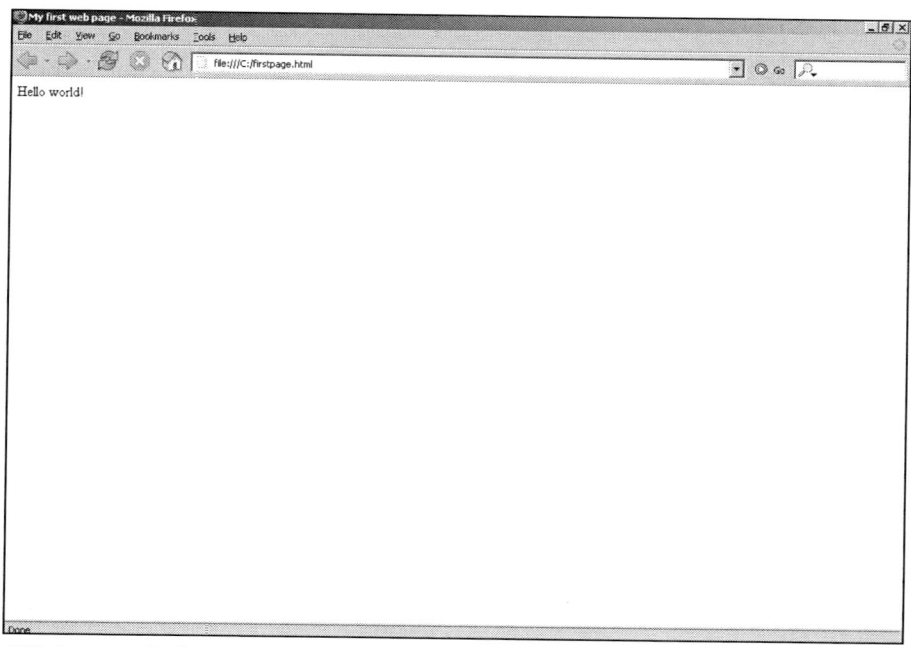

Web browser displaying the result of the HTML code on page 92

> **Tip**
> You might want to create a new folder for your HTML files. Open up the My Files folder, then right click and select New > Folder. This will create a new folder within the My Files folder. Give it a sensible name like "HTML files". Now you can save all your HTML files within this folder and you'll always know where to find them.

You've just written your first HTML page – congratulations! Now let's look at what the HTML document consists of. You're probably wondering what the funny things in the angular brackets '< >' are. These are called tags, and basically they tell your browser what to do with your text. For example:

```
<TITLE>My first web page</TITLE>
```

tells the browser that this document has a title, and that the title is "My first web page". Notice that the title is only that text contained within the two title tags.

Most tags have a start tag and an end tag which defines their sphere of influence e.g. <TITLE> </TITLE>. (Notice that the end tag has a slash after the first bracket – don't forget this slash or the page won't display correctly.) So the <HTML> tags at the start and end of your page tell your browser that this is an HTML document and it should interpret the other tags accordingly.

HTML documents generally have two parts: a head and a body. The head is enclosed by the <HEAD> tags, and includes information about the document such as its title. The main body of the document is enclosed by, you guessed it, the <BODY> tags. (We told you this was easy.) This is where your page's content goes.

As we mentioned earlier, the page's title is enclosed between <TITLE> tags, within the document's head. This is what is shown at the top of the browser when you visit a page (for example in the blue bar at the top of the Internet Explorer window). Try changing the text between the title tags, save your altered page in Notepad (just go to File then Save). Now refresh the page in your browser by clicking on the refresh or reload button. (In Internet Explorer you can also refresh the page simply by pressing the F5 key.) Notice that the title has changed? Try changing the text between the <BODY> tags. Remember to save the page in Notepad and refresh the page in the browser each time, or you won't see any difference.

Now let's look at some more tags. Change the text between the body tags to the following. (Don't touch the rest of the page.)

```
<BODY>
<B>This is in bold.</B><BR>
<I>This is in italics.</I><BR>
<U>This is underlined.</U><BR>
</BODY>
```

Save the file and refresh your browser window. It should be clear what the <B>, <I> and <U> tags do. You'll notice that the <BR> tag puts in a line break i.e. it makes the next piece of text start on a new line. This is important because the browser usually ignores any return characters you have in your HTML file. For example, you might write a text such as the following as part of your HTML file, creating each new line by pressing the return key (as you would do in a word processor):

```
...
<BODY>
It is an ancient Mariner,
And he stoppeth one of three.
"By thy long grey beard and glittering eye,
Now wherefore stopp'st thou me?
</BODY>
...
```

But if you were to view this in your browser, you would be aghast to see it rendered as one continuous line – hardly what Coleridge intended. To get the presentation right, you have to put a <BR> tag at the end of each line:

```
...
<BODY>
It is an ancient Mariner,<BR>
And he stoppeth one of three.<BR>
"By thy long grey beard and glittering eye,<BR>
Now wherefore stopp'st thou me?<BR>
</BODY>
...
```

Adding the
 (line break tag) solves the problem.

8

Creating Your Own Website

Now, it wouldn't be hypertext without hyperlinks, so let's look at the link tag next. For this we're going to create two pages, each linked to the other. Open up another Notepad by going to Start > Programs > Accessories. (Remember you can have several different Notepads and browser windows open at any one time. Remember also that you can easily switch between programs in Windows by clicking on the little rectangles along the bottom of your screen, or pressing ALT and the tab key.)

In the first Notepad, write the following:

```
<HTML>
<HEAD>
<TITLE>Page one</TITLE>
</HEAD>
<BODY>
This is page one.<BR>
<A HREF="pagetwo.html">Go to page two.</A>
</BODY>
</HTML>
```

Save this file as pageone.html. Remember where you saved it.

In the second Notepad, write this:

```
<HTML>
<HEAD>
<TITLE>Page two</TITLE>
</HEAD>
<BODY>
This is page two.<BR>
<A HREF="pageone.html">Go to page one.</A>
</BODY>
</HTML>
```

(You may want to copy and paste the text from the other page to speed things up – see the Appendix on keyboard-shortcuts to help you with this.)

Save this as pagetwo.html, in the same folder (very important!) as pageone.html. Now go to your browser and open up pageone.html. Lo and behold, you'll see the familiar blue underlined link saying "Go to page two." Click on the link and page two should appear, assuming there are no typos in your HTML files. Clicking on the link here will bring you back to page one. And so on, to your heart's content.

(If the links don't work, check that you've typed the text exactly as it appears here. Also check that you've saved both files, and that you've saved them in the same folder. Remember to choose All Files (*.*) for Save As Type when you're saving the files.)

Once you've grown tired of switching between page one and page two, take another look at the hyperlink tag. (It's actually called an anchor tag, hence the A.) Whatever gets enclosed between the start and end <A> tags turns into a hyperlink. The HREF= "..." bit tells the browser where to go when the link is clicked on. Here it's just the name of a file. The browser assumes that this file is in the same folder as the page with the link. This is useful for linking pages within your site.

But what if you want to link to a page outside your site? Easy. Simply add this line to pageone.html:

    <A HREF="http://www.google.com">Google</A>

Save the page, then refresh your browser window. Now you have a link to

> **Tip**
> Novice web designers often wonder if it's acceptable to link to another site without permission. Normally the answer is yes. After all, you're potentially providing more visitors for that site – the site's owner is hardly likely to complain. The only case where you might run into problems is if you're using 'frames'. Frames are a way to divide up a web page into different sections, each of which shows a different HTML file – for example you might have your menu in one frame, and the main content in a second frame. If you're using frames and you link to a site in such a way that it looks like it's part of your site, rather than an external website, then site's owner's might object.

the search engine Google. If you click on this link then you will switch to the Google home page (assuming you're online, of course). To link to a different site, simply change the address between the quotation marks. Don't forget the http:// bit or it won't work.

Let's look at one more very useful tag, the image tag. You use this to incorporate graphics within your page. First of all, find an image on your hard drive. Look for the file extensions .jpg, .gif or .png to identify image files. These represent the file formats JPEG, GIF and PNG, the three most common file formats used on the web. You don't need to worry about the differences between them at this stage.

If you don't know where to find any images, go to Start > Find > Files or Folders. Type *.jpg into the search window next to Named, and choose C: for the Look In option, then click on Find Now. You'll get a list of all the JPEG images on your hard drive. Click on one of these images, then right-click to get the context menu, and select copy. Then, using Windows Explorer, go to the folder where you've been saving your HTML files and paste the image into it, again by right clicking and selecting paste from the context menu.

Let's say you've got a JPEG image of your pet dog, Boris. The file is called boris.jpg. Add this line to pageone.html:

```
<IMG SRC="boris.jpg">
```

Change the file name (the bit between the quotation marks) to the name of the image you wish to use.

Save the file and then look at the result in your browser. Hopefully you should see a picture of little Boris, or whatever your chosen image contains. If all you get is a square with an X in it, check that the image file is in the same folder as your HTML file, and that you spelled the file name correctly. Also check that you've got lower/upper-case correct as this can make a difference.

> **Tip**
> When designing your web page, make sure that each web page has a link back to the start page or the page that links to it. It's considered bad form to have an 'orphan page' with no links, forcing your visitor to use the back button on the browser to get out.

> **Tip**
> Many web designers like to use images as links, because they look more attractive than plain text. However, be aware that there are people surfing the web who cannot see images (people who have images switched off in their browsers, or blind people, for example). If you do decide to use an image as a link, make sure you have an equivalent text link to accommodate text-only users.

You've probably already worked out that IMG is short for 'image'. SRC means 'source', and tells your browser where to find the image file. Notice that you don't need an end tag for image tags.

Often web designers like to keep all their images in a separate folder within their site, for convenience. If you want to do this, create a new folder within your HTML files folder, and call it 'Media' (or whatever). Move your image file into this folder, then change the image tag to read:

```
<IMG SRC="Media/boris.jpg">
```

The 'Media/' bit tells the browser to look in the sub-folder Media to find the boris.jpg file. You can make an image into a link simply by putting it inside anchor tags. To try this, change the link in your pageone.html file to:

```
<A HREF="pagetwo.html"><IMG SRC="boris.jpg"></A>
```

If you look at your page you will see that your image of Boris is now the link. If you put the pointer over the image, it will turn into the familiar little hand, and clicking on the image will take you to pagetwo.html.

This short tutorial should be enough to give you a flavour of HTML and what it can do. Should you be interested, there's lots more to learn about the delights of HTML. The easiest way is probably to buy a book on HTML – look for a title like 'Beginning HTML' or similar. The publishers Wrox and O'Reilly are both very respected, and you won't go wrong with any of their publications. Make sure you check that the book has been published recently, preferably within the last couple of years; the internet moves at such a pace that information more than a couple of years old is often already out of date. Alternatively, there are dozens, if not hundreds, of HTML tutorials online such as the excellent Maricopa Writing HTML tutorial; if nothing else, the

8

Creating Your Own Website

web is a great place to learn about the web. Simply do a search for 'HTML tutorial' in a search engine and you'll get thousands of hits. (Or look in the Appendix for some suggestions.)

Alternatives to HTML

As mentioned before, HTML is just a formatting language. That means that it's relatively simple to learn and use. However once you start doing your own web pages, you may find HTML too limited for what you really want to do. Let's say you want to have a multiple-choice language exercise on your page where learners have to complete sentences by choosing the right word from four options, and you want the page to tell them if their answers are correct or not. Unfortunately plain HTML is just not up to the job. There are various ways to lend interactivity to your website, with one of the most popular ways being to use JavaScript. JavaScript is a programming language specifically designed for web pages. (Incidentally, it bears very little relation to the well-known programming language Java – the similarity in the names was a mere marketing ploy.) Many of the interactive language exercises you'll find on the web are written in JavaScript. JavaScript would allow you to write the hypothetical language exercise described above.

Unfortunately, covering JavaScript is outside the scope of this book. If you do decide to learn JavaScript (and it is definitely worth the effort), you might want to buy a book, or consult some of the many online tutorials. Search for `JavaScript tutorial` in your favourite search engine, or look at the appendices for some suggestions. JavaScript will take you significantly longer to learn than HTML – whereas HTML can be learned in an afternoon, you will probably need 10-15 hours to master the basics of JavaScript, more if you've never seen a programming language before.

> **Jargon Box**
> Authoring software such as Hot Potatoes (see Chapter 9 on authoring software for more information) normally create pages which use JavaScript, meaning you don't have to be familiar with JavaScript yourself to include such exercises in your website.

However, there is a quick and dirty alternative to learning JavaScript. Here's a simple way to add JavaScript interactivity to your web page without knowing anything about JavaScript itself. First of all, find a page on the web which does the thing you want to do, for example a multiple-choice exercise. Look at the source code by doing View > Source, then save the source code to your hard drive by selecting Save As. Now change the content of the page (i.e. the text and pictures) to suit your needs. Be careful about changing bits which you don't understand! Alternatively copy the important sections of JavaScript and HTML into your web page. The important JavaScript parts are normally in the head of the start of the page, inside <SCRIPT> tags, and in the body of the page between <FORM> tags. With a bit of trial and error, and a bit of luck, you should be able to alter the page to suit your needs. And there's no need for a guilty conscience as a result of swiping someone else's work – web designers do this all the time. (But don't re-use the content of the page without the owner's permission – this is definitely not allowed.) If you're curious to find out more about JavaScript, take a look at the code and see if you can figure out how it works – this is a great way to teach yourself.

If you really get into web design (and many language teachers seem to, if our circle of acquaintances is anything to go by) then at some point you're going to find even JavaScript limited. Then you'll probably want to learn a heavy-duty web programming language such as ASP.NET (from Microsoft) or PHP (the open source alternative), and maybe XML in addition. Be warned – these are not for the faint-hearted. However, they will allow you to do some really clever stuff on your website; many professional websites use these technologies. Again, these languages are outside the scope of this book, but they are definitely worth bearing in mind as your skills and interest deepen.

Another option for interactive exercises which doesn't involve learning a programming language is to use Flash. You've probably seen Flash sites on the web already. It's a program from the company Macromedia which allows you to combine moving and stationary pictures with sound and interactivity. You can use it to create some very nice-looking websites including, for example, multiple-choice quizzes or drag and drop exercises.

However there are a couple of drawbacks to using Flash. First of all, you have to buy the software from Macromedia, and it doesn't come cheap. Then there's the steep learning curve involved, even though in some ways it's easier than learning a programming language because you do everything via a 'point and click' interface – you don't need to get your hands dirty. The other disadvantage of using Flash is that Flash sites are normally quite big and therefore need a long time to load, especially with slow connections. This could be a problem if your learners only have modems, for example. On the other hand, Flash sites can be very attractive and sexy, in a way that plain old HTML seldom is. And you won't have any compatibility problems – your site will look pretty much the same in every browser. This is in marked contrast to HTML, where the same code will be displayed slightly – or even very – differently in each different browser version.

Getting your page online

Okay, so now you've created a wonderful website, with several different pages all linked together, some nice images, and links to the best websites the web can offer. The only problem is it's still stuck on your hard drive where no one else can see it. You need to get it out there on the web where your creation can be admired in all its glory.

One thing which is crucial to understand is that no one can access the web pages if they're simply sitting on your hard drive. Instead, the pages have to be on a web server. This is a special kind of computer which is always connected to the internet. When you type a URL like www.google.com into your browser, your browser contacts the server which that URL refers to, and asks it to send particular files (for example, the Google home page) to your browser. The web server then sends copies of the files from its hard drive to your own computer, where you can view them. Similarly, if you want to publish your web pages on the internet, you have to upload your files from your home computer to a particular web server, where other people can access them by typing the appropriate URL into their browser. (As it happens, you could actually turn your home computer into a web server if you really wanted to, but that's probably a little ambitious for the moment.)

Tripod and GeoCities

Possibly the easiest way to establish a web presence is to get a free website with <u>Lycos</u> or <u>Yahoo</u>!, whose services are called <u>Tripod</u> and <u>GeoCities</u> respectively. If you've done a bit of surfing on the web, you've probably come across sites belonging to both services at some point. (They normally have little ads that pop up with Tripod or GeoCities written on them.) If all you want is a simple web page to, say, set homework for a particular class, then this is an easy way to do it.

At the time of writing, both services give you free web space, although you might have to look hard on their websites to find the free options – they are usually displayed in much smaller writing than the paid options. The only catch with the free web space is the ads on your site, proving that there is in fact no such thing as a free lunch. (If you don't want ads, you can pay a monthly fee instead.) You also have to join Lycos or Yahoo! in order to use the service – this involves creating a user name and password for yourself, which should only take a couple of minutes. Read the options carefully when you complete the form and be careful which boxes you check, otherwise you'll end up receiving piles of email newsletters you might not want.

One of the good things about both services is that they are aimed at a range of users, from beginners to experienced web designers. So if you've never produced a web page before, they offer templates which will ask you a few questions regarding content and layout, then create pages from your input. Naturally pages created from the default options tend to look a bit samey, but you can always edit the pages later to make them more interesting.

If you have a little more experience, or are feeling more ambitious, you can use other tools to edit your web pages. Again, both services offer a range of options: you can use a user-friendly point and click interface, or you can edit the HTML code directly. (Let us just repeat here that learning a bit of HTML is really worth the effort.)

You can also upload files from your hard drive to the Tripod or GeoCities web space. These files could be for example HTML documents which you've written yourself, or images you want to use on your site. This is done via an interface on the Tripod or GeoCities website. You simply choose a file from the folders on your computer, click on the Upload button and they are transferred to the web server. Then you can edit your web pages to either link to the new HTML documents or include the images in your page. Naturally there's a limit to how much space you can occupy on the Tripod or GeoCities server, but for a simple web page there's little danger of going over your allocation.

And that's it. With a bit of luck you should be able to have a simple web page up and running with either of these services within an hour or so.

(Just in passing, we'd like to mention that Lycos also has a website called Webmonkey which has some of the best, not to mention wittiest, web design tutorials on the web. It's a great place to hone your web design skills.)

Getting your own web space

But what if you don't want to go down the Lycos/Yahoo! road? There are plenty of other alternatives. You might well have some web space already and not even know it – many ISPs offer web space as part of their package. For example, as part of David's deal with Snafu, a local ISP in his chosen hometown of Berlin, he gets 10MB of web space in addition to his internet connection and email address. If you're not sure if your ISP gives you free web space, take another look at their web page or your contract, or give their hotline a call. (They do have a hotline, don't they? If not, you should maybe think about switching to an ISP with better customer service.)

If your ISP doesn't give you web space as part of the deal, then you will need a web hosting company. A web hosting company (or web host) rents out web space to customers. For a monthly fee, you get a certain amount of space on a web server. There are literally thousands of web hosting companies out there, so how do you choose which one to go for? The simplest way (even if it does sound a bit low tech) is probably to ask one of your web-savvy friends – preferably one with their own website – which they would recommend.

Don't have any web-savvy friends? One option might be to find a personal website belonging to someone who seems to know what they're doing, and simply write them an email asking them which web host they use. (IT people are good to ask because they normally know what they're talking about.)

> **Jargon box**
> An ISP or Internet Service Provider is a company which provides access to the internet, allowing you to send and receive email and browse the web.

The alternative is to do a bit of research on the internet. See the Appendix for some ideas for where to start. One tip – you might want to choose a web hosting company located in the country where you live. Among other advantages, it makes it easier to get hold of them by phone should problems arise. And remember that with web hosting, like many things, you get what you pay for. Reliability and service are worth shelling out a bit more for, especially if your site is business-related – you don't want your site to be inaccessible when a key customer is trying to visit it.

Uploading pages to a web server

Now, if you have web space with your ISP or a web host, you will have to upload your pages via FTP (which stands for File Transfer Protocol), rather than with a browser a la Tripod and GeoCities. This will involve learning to use a new piece of software, but don't worry, it's not that difficult. Normally your ISP or web host will have a help page on their website which explains how to do this, and you should definitely read that. However, here is some information to get you started.

First of all, you're going to have to get your hands on an FTP program. This is easy – you can download free FTP software from the internet. Many people use CuteFTP from GlobalSCAPE or WS_FTP from Ipswitch, which both have free versions of their software at the time of writing. Quite possibly you can download an FTP program directly from your ISP/web host website. To download and install the software, simply follow the instructions on the site you are downloading the software from.

The idea behind FTP software is very simple. The FTP program creates a connection between your home PC and your web server, and allows you to transfer files from your hard drive to the server and vice versa. Normally an

Creating Your Own Website

FTP program has two windows, one which shows the folders and files on your hard drive, and the other which shows the folders and files on your web server. (Generally you are only allowed to look at the folders and files in your own personal web space on the server, for obvious reasons.)

When you start your FTP program, it will ask you for your server's FTP address, your login name and your password. You will have been given these things by your ISP or web host – you've probably got them on a piece of paper somewhere. Type these in, then press the ok or connect button. The program will then connect you to your web server. You'll see a screen which looks something like the one on page 106.

The box on the left shows the folders and files on your hard drive, and the box on the right shows what's on your web space. If you want to transfer a file from your computer to the web server, select a file from the left box by clicking on it, then click on the right-pointing arrow button. Hey presto – a copy of the file gets sent to the web server. (The program even makes a little

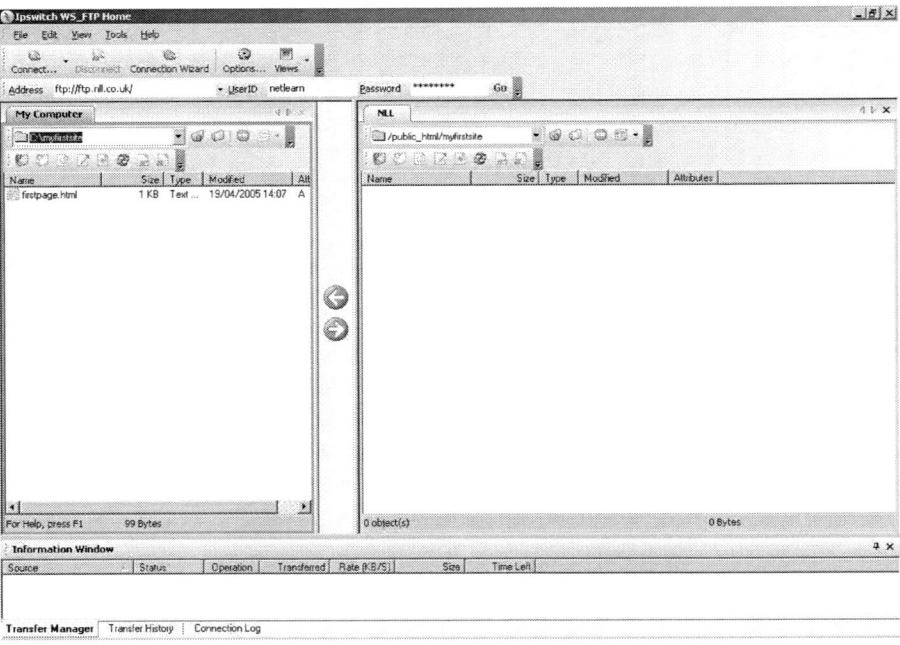

The FTP program WS_FTP from Ipswitch

106

noise to tell you that the file has been sent successfully.) If you want to transfer a file from your web space to your hard drive, just click on the appropriate file in the right window, then click on the left-facing button. Easy! Naturally there's a lot more you can do with your FTP program should you want to, but that's enough to get you started.

Looking at your pages online

Once you have transferred your website files to your web space, you will want to look at your pages in a browser, if for no other reason than to check that everything works. (It's very easy to forget to upload a crucial page or image, or you might find that a link which worked on your hard drive no longer goes anywhere.) To look at your newly-uploaded pages, you simply type the appropriate URL into your web browser. Your ISP or web host will have given you this information. If you don't have your own domain name (more about that later) then the URL will probably look something like http://home.snafu.de/david.smith/. This is actually a link to the folder which is your web space. If you type this URL into your browser, it will either show a list of the files which you have uploaded to your web space, or it will tell you that you are not allowed to view the files, or it will display the default web page, which is probably called index.html, if you have uploaded a file with the appropriate name.

You can access specific pages within your site by adding the name of the file after the name of the folder. For example, if David wanted to access a file called teaching.htm within his web space, he would type http://home.snafu.de/david.smith/teaching.htm into the address field.

> **Tip**
> Your ISP will have told you the name of the default or start page on your web space. It's a good idea to always have a file with this name on your web space. For one thing, you need a page for your visitors to start from. Also, you don't really want your visitors to be able to see all the files you have stored in your space.

Getting a domain name

So now you have a website loaded on to a web server, which anyone can access. Congratulations! There's only one problem: your current web address (which looks something like http://home.snafu.de/david.smith/) is neither very memorable nor sexy. Depending on what you need a website for, this arbitrary address may be enough, especially considering that domain names are not free. If, however, you want your website to have a more professional image, you will need to get yourself a domain name. And remember that most people expect websites to have domain names these days.

Before you actually register your domain name, you will have to decide which domain name you want for your site. While opinions differ on what makes a good domain name, it's safe to say that a domain name should be easy for visitors to remember and type, not too long, and somehow related to the content of your site. You might wish to make a shortlist of your preferred names, in case your first choice is not available.

At this stage you should also think about which TLD (e.g. .com, .co.uk etc) you want for your domain name. While .com extensions are allegedly more prestigious, it's often more difficult to find a good .com name which is available, compared to less common TLDs like .biz. If your website is directed mainly at visitors from one country (presumably your country of residence) you may decide to go for a country code TLD like .de or .fr. Again, your dream name is more likely to be available with a country code TLD than with an international TLD. In addition, the actual process of registering the domain may be simpler if you stick to your local country code domain. Speaking from personal experience, we found getting a .de or a .co.uk domain name much less work than getting a .com domain.

> **Tip**
> You are probably already familiar with domain names from visiting websites. They look like www.google.com or www.snafu.de. The last part of the name is called the top level domain or TLD. Examples of TLDs include .com, .org, .net, .biz, and .info. Two-letter TLDs for countries, such as .de for Germany or .fr for France, are referred to as country code TLDs or ccTLDs.

Once you've made a short list of possible names, the next step is to see if they are available. To do this, you will have to search for your name in a WHOIS directory. If you want an international TLD like .com, .org etc, you can search in the WHOIS database on the InterNIC website. Simply type in your desired name (e.g. davidsmith.com or ericbaber.com), click on submit and it will tell you if your domain is already taken or not. You can do the same thing for domains with country code TLDs at the Uwhois website.

Once you've found a name which you like and which is available, you now have to register it. If you are a novice, or if you simply want an easy life, we would recommend that you let your ISP or web host handle the dirty work of registering the domain name. Generally they have a page on their website where you simply tell them which domain you want and they'll do the rest. Your ISP or web host will tell you once your domain name has been registered, and you will find that you can now either type your original default web address (like http://home.snafu.de/david.smith/) or your new domain name (e.g. www.davidsmithhomepage.com) to view your site. You will also now be able to create email addresses with your domain e.g. david.smith@davidsmithhomepage.com. Naturally you will have to pay your ISP or web host for this service, but it shouldn't cost too much.

The only problem with getting your ISP or web host to register the domain name, is that it is not unheard of for unscrupulous companies to register the name in such a way that you will have difficulties in transferring it to another ISP or web host, should you choose to switch provider. Basically if you want to maintain complete autonomy over your domain, you'll have to register it yourself.

This is slightly more technical. If you want an international domain name like .com, you have to choose a registrar from the many companies which are authorised to register these TLDs. The ICANN website has a list of accredited registrars. Choose a registrar then follow the instructions on their website to register your domain.

If you want to have a domain with a country-code TLD, then you first have to visit the IANA website to find which company is responsible for registering domains with your chosen TLD. There is one company responsible for each ccTLD – for example, in Germany a company called DENIC is responsible for .de domains. Once you have found the appropriate company for your TLD, you have to visit their website and follow the instructions there to register your domain name.

Publicising your website

Once you've got your domain name and web space, you're all set! Now it's simply a question of letting people know about your site. Send emails to your friends telling them about it. Put your URL into your email signature and write to lots of mailing lists so that people see it. Trade links with other relevant sites (write to them and offer to link to their site if they link to yours). Register your site with the major search engines, or wait for them to find you (the likelihood of which depends largely on how many sites link to your site). Then sit back and wait for the praise and adulation (or complaints and random questions, if our experience is anything to go by) to come flooding in!

Conclusion

You might want to have your own website if you:

- are running your own business or are a freelancer and would like (potential) clients to be able to find out about your services;
- want to make information or exercises available on the web for existing students and want complete control over how your students can access your materials;
- would like to be able to offer blended-learning courses, consisting of face-to-face instruction backed up by online exercises;
- want to be able to help your students set up their own website as a project.

Chapter 9

Authoring Software: Creating Interactive Exercises

You've seen other ELT websites with fantastic interactive exercises on them. You've learnt a bit of HTML and have done some basic websites. Now you want to do your own great interactive exercises. The bad new is, your HTML knowledge isn't enough – for interactive exercises you need to know other programming languages such as JavaScript. The good news is there are other ways of producing interactive exercises without having to learn a new programming language. The easiest option is to use an authoring software, namely a software which will help you create interactive exercises without the tears.

There are various options available to the aspiring exercise writer. For example, you can:

- Download software from the Internet (or buy it on CD), install it on your computer, and use it to create individual exercises or complete web pages. You can then publish these on your website, put them on the computer(s) at your school for your students, or use them in any other way you like.

- Visit a website which will create the exercise for you, which you then save to your hard drive. Again you can then upload exercises to your web

server and integrate them in with the rest of your site, or else use them only on your computers at school.
- Create your exercise on the website and also store it there, so students have to visit that particular website to do the exercise. Naturally you can link from your site (if you have one) directly to the exercise you've made on the other site, thereby making it easier for your students to find the exercises you've made.

We should also mention in passing that with this kind of software you can usually print out the exercises on paper, as well as creating HTML pages. This can be handy if, for example, all you want to do is create a crossword to use in class. Letting your authoring software figure out the crossword for you certainly beats trying to do it yourself!

There are dozens of authoring software programs available, many of which are freeware or shareware. You can easily find out about the latest authoring software by doing a search for, for example, `authoring software`, `interactive exercises`, `worksheet generator` English in your favourite search engine. To give you an idea of what is possible, we will take a look at two popular authoring softwares, one which you install on your computer (Hot Potatoes) and one which you use via the web (Quia).

Hot Potatoes

Hot Potatoes is probably the most popular authoring software among language teachers (as well as teachers of a range of other subjects). It's been around for several years and has gone through several versions. It is produced by Half-Baked Software Inc (how these IT people love their puns).

You can download Hot Potatoes for free (provided you are intending to use it for non-profit purposes) from the Hot Potatoes home page. Once you've installed it you can use it to make your own exercises. At the time of writing there are six different kinds of exercises available:

    1. Multiple choices quizzes;

    2. Short answer quizzes;

    3. Jumbled sentence quizzes;

9

Authoring Software

4. Crossword puzzles;

5. Matching exercises;

6. Fill-in-the-blanks exercises.

Hot Potatoes provides you with a user-friendly interface which takes the hard work out of producing exercises. For example, to make a crossword exercise, you simply type in the list of words you want to include in your crossword, and the program makes a grid accommodating all those words. Then you assign a clue to each word, press the 'export to Web' button, and the program automatically produces a web page with your crossword. You can then send this HTML file to your students by email, transfer it to their machines by saving it on a floppy disk which you then give to them, or upload it to your website.

There are, as always, a couple of snags with Hot Potatoes, despite its many virtues. One is that, like any piece of software, it takes a while to learn how to use it properly, although the tutorial and help functions are very useful.

Another potential drawback is that you are limited in the ways you can customise the exercise (presumably to avoid overloading the novice user with choices). So for example with the jumbled sentence exercise, you can only have one sentence per exercise. Considering it will might take a student only ten seconds to un-jumble any particular sentence, the exercise will not last very long.

On a similar note, Hot Potatoes exercises generally look very 'Hot Potatoes' i.e. they are instantly recognisable as having been created with this software. This will probably not be a problem, unless you might want to sell your exercises (having first obtained the correct licence, of course) and don't want a potential customer to know that you have used Hot Potatoes to create the exercises. Having said that, if your HTML skills are somewhat more advanced, you can alter the look and feel of the pages generated by Hot Potatoes to match that of the rest of your website, or to adapt it to the website of your client (if you are selling the materials you have created to a customer).

The other fly in the ointment is compatibility with different browsers. Hot Potatoes, along with other puzzle-making packages, allows you to create snazzy drag and drop exercises using DHTML. We don't need to go into what exactly DHTML is – suffice to say that it can be used to make some

Hot Potatoes

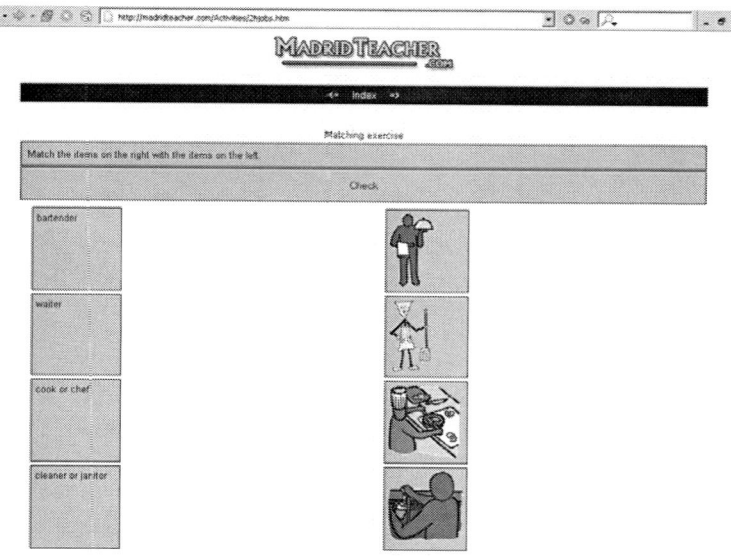

A Hot Potatoes matching exercise

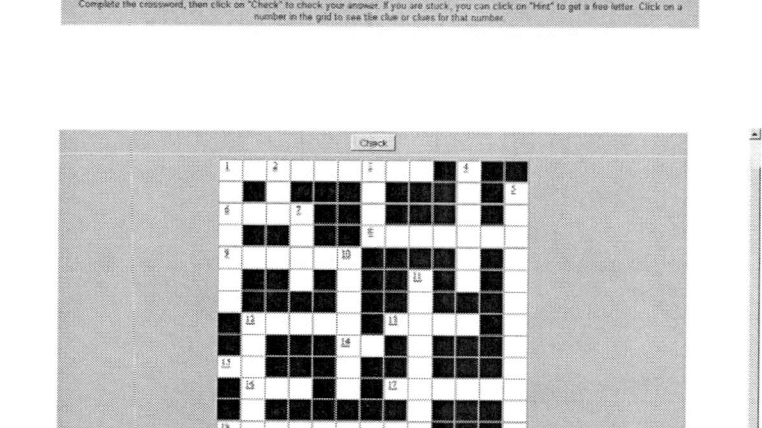

A crossword made with Hot Potatoes

Authoring Software

very slick effects, such as clicking on a box and dragging it with the mouse over to another box (which might not sound very impressive, but is still a lot more exciting than selecting the right answer from a drop-down menu). The first time we saw this in Hot Potatoes we thought 'Great! Why isn't the Web full of cool stuff like this?' There's a simple reason – incompatibility. It's very difficult to write DHTML pages which will work on different browsers. If you've created a page which works in the latest version of Internet Explorer, and all your students are using that same version, you're fine. But a page which works with Explorer may not necessarily work with Netscape, and vice versa. And anyone with an older browser can forget it.

Basically this means that you have to choose with care how many bells and whistles to use. With Hot Potatoes for example, you can choose which 'version' you want your output page to be in. If you choose, say, 'version 3', then your page will work with most browsers people are likely to have these days, but it will be fairly basic in terms of interactivity. But choosing 'version 5' for your output means that your carefully-crafted exercise can only be viewed by someone with an up-to-date browser. So think carefully about who your target audience is, and which browsers they are likely to be using. If in doubt, go for a more basic version.

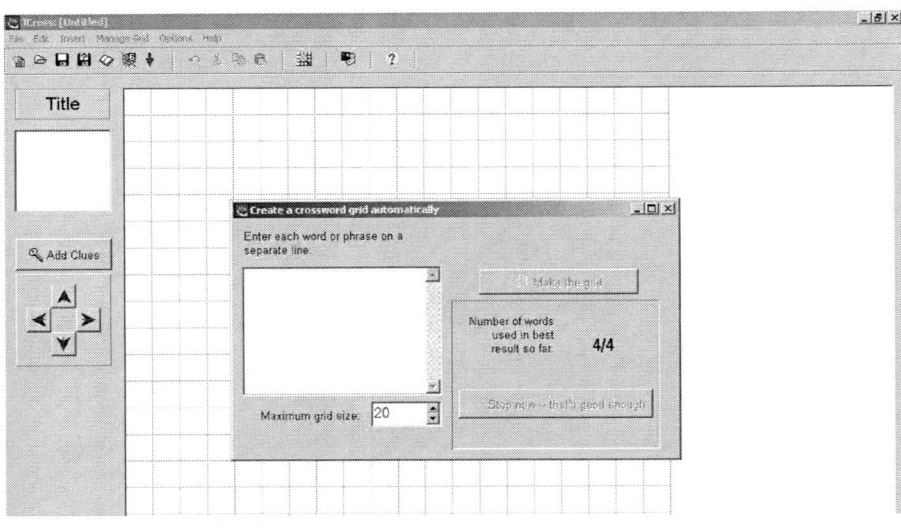

Creating a crossword with Hot Potatoes

On the whole though, Hot Potatoes is an excellent piece of software which is justifiably popular with the teaching community and is well worth investigating.

Quia

The other option for creating interactive exercises is to use a web-based service. One of the most popular of these websites is Quia.com (pronounced 'key-ah'). This site allows educators to create activities and quizzes over the Internet and share them with others, to give online quizzes and track students' scores, and to create their own Web pages for posting assignments,

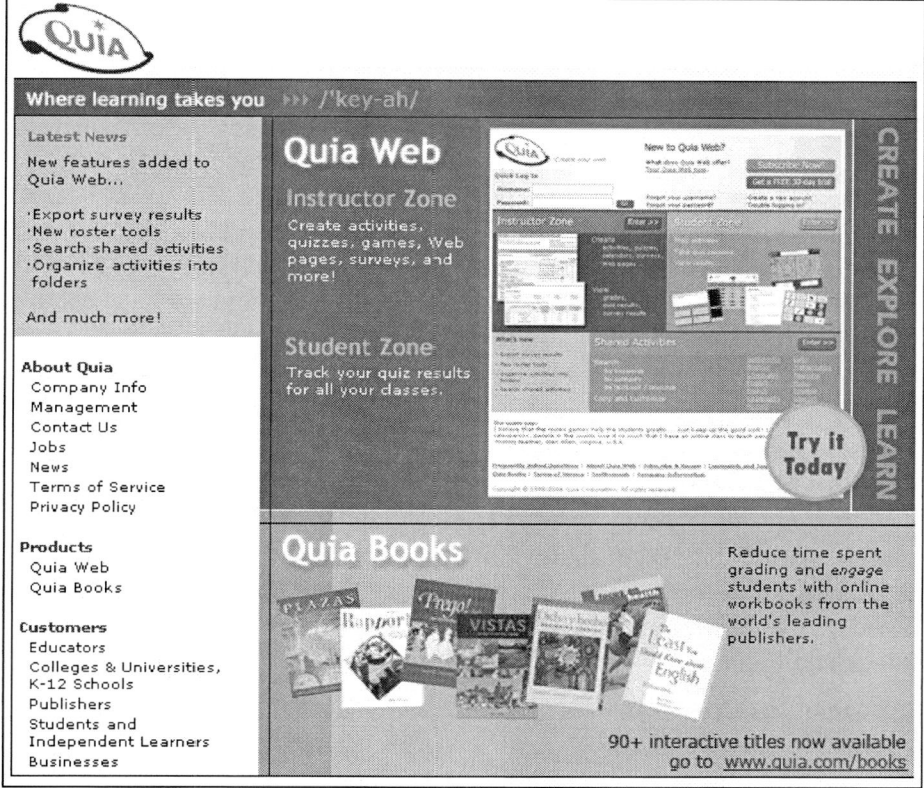

The Quia web-based service

9

Authoring Software

and class schedules. Anyone can visit the site and do exercises from a selection of thousands already created by other teachers. The quality of the exercises available varies enormously, as you might expect, but there are certainly plenty relevant for English language teaching.

If you wish to create your own exercises, you will need to subscribe. At the time of writing, a free 30-day trial subscription is available, with a one-year subscription costing US$49.

Once you have subscribed, you are free to create class pages, quizzes etc to your heart's content. Creating content is very straightforward, with the web page giving you templates to complete and asking you in plain English about your preferences regarding layout etc.

Once a page has been completed, the site gives you a permanent URL (web address) for that page, which you can then pass on to your students and colleagues. You can also choose to enter your exercises in the Quia directory, which means that random strangers can also benefit from your hard work. Creating a class page allows you to structure the exercises you have created, as well as setting assignments, giving your students useful links, etc. It's also possible to link to your exercises from an outside website. However, it's not possible to save the exercises so you can use them offline or as pages on a different website, so doing the exercises always involves visiting the Quia site. You may see this as a drawback if you wish your exercises to be an integral part of your own site. It also means that students have to be online to do the exercises (as opposed to say Hot Potatoes, which produces HTML pages which can be used offline).

An impressive range of 14 exercise types are available, including matching exercises, hangman, clozes, quizzes and various games. Like most puzzle-makers, your options are limited in terms of layout and how the exercises work. This certainly keeps things simple, and means you can create exercises in a couple of minutes, but could prove frustrating in the long run. Students could also find the constant repetition tedious. This is of course a criticism which applies to all puzzle-making software.

In conclusion, Quia is an easy way to create interactive exercises for your students to access over the web. However the price you pay for the convenience it offers is limited flexibility in how you use those exercises.

Using interactive exercises

So how can you integrate web-based interactive exercises into your language teaching? Here are some examples of ways you can use them.

Let's say you teach a group of students once a week. You could create an interactive exercise using, for example, Hot Potatoes each week to revise material covered in that week's lesson. You could upload the exercise to your own website (you might have a separate section on your website especially for that particular group) and get the students to do it for homework. Or you could send it to the students by email as an attachment. By the end of the course, the students will have a comprehensive series of exercises covering the material they have met in the lessons. At the end of the course you could burn all the exercises onto a CD-ROM and give a copy to each student so that they can continue to practise their English after the course.

Alternatively, you might be teaching Business English in a company. In this situation, you could create a special website specifically for that company, featuring interactive exercises. Ideally this would be located on the company intranet, to make it easy for employees to use it. (This would normally involve speaking to the IT people in the company to find out if such a website was feasible.) This is an ideal way to provide a company with a 'value-added' extra as a way of giving yourself the edge on the competition. Of course, if you are smart/mercenary you could even charge them for it. One possibility would be to do a needs analysis for the whole company (a so-called 'language audit') and then prepare exercises addressing the needs of different groups of students. For example, you could write telephoning exercises for the secretarial staff, or small-talk exercises for the managers. The exercises could be organised in different sections on your intranet website. You might also want to combine this with a daily email to all employees featuring interesting words, useful phrases etc.

Of course, you might also want to create a website with English language exercises on the public internet, for the benefit of all humanity. This would involve getting web space and a domain name and writing HTML pages (see the chapter on creating a website for more details) and adding your exercises to the site. If you are going to do this, please give careful thought to which

Authoring Software

exercises you are going to write and how you are going to organise them – there are already too many websites with a limited selection of random exercises. Try to organise your exercises into something akin to a syllabus, covering different language areas in a comprehensive fashion, in order to provide the maximum benefit to learners. If you are really clever you might even be able to charge people for using your exercises, but at the time of writing this is unlikely due to the sheer amount of free material available on the web.

Conclusion

You should consider using authoring software if the following statements are true for you:

- you want to create interactive exercises to publish on the internet;
- you want to create interactive exercises to complement your face-to-face teaching;
- you have basic computer skills and don't mind learning to use new software;
- you don't mind if the interactive exercises you create are limited in terms of design and functionality (if you do, then the best thing is to learn JavaScript or Flash).

Chapter 10

Using Standalone Software

As well as all the internet-specific applications and software which have been covered in previous chapters, it is also possible to use standalone PC software to help your students learn English. In this chapter we'll be looking at how you can integrate concordancers, audio software and office packages into your teaching. Of course there are many more programs that could be used for learning English – with some imagination you can probably turn most of the software you have on your PC into teaching or learning tools.

Concordancers

A concordancer is one of the most useful tools a language teacher (or student) can have.

Simply put, a concordancer is a software program which allows you to analyse how particular words are used in a text or texts. It does this by producing a 'concordance' for a given search term. Turn the page to see what the output of a concordance looks like:

10

Using Standalone Software

```
      are a lot things he hasn't kept his word about. We just want everybody out. I'
   tell her if she ever even breathes a word about baby-sitting again you'll tell
over.Neary: This has come down to his word against hers, and I think everybody
        ability to use the consonants in a word along with the context is an
       church where she was enclosed. The word anchoress is a cognate of a Greek
          analogue audio, 2xbnc for video, word, and digital audio sync. Outputs:
     however, often take people at their word and can occasionally be rather
           and obvious in so far as the very word 'antique' derives from Greek
  p] She said it as if it were a dirty word. At last something that Mary and I
   broken. Mashed seemed the appropriate word at the time.  [p] Uppermost in my
       has a Vice-President who can use the word `Cartesian" in place of one who
         bars of `Sheela-Na-Gig' get echoed word for word, and Rob and Steve are
           Afghans call it Khad, the Persian word for secret service, although it
     a good keeper and the gaffer took my word for it.  [p] We want quality at this
              known. Lower down the slopes, the word from cabinet members is of the
  man of peace in Northern Ireland. His word has been accepted almost without
   is not obvious by looking at the root word. Have students set up their papers
    day in his life. In 1900, true to his word, he rescued the doctor's 175-acre
          Pan group had associations to the word `hook" which the Robinson Crusoe
              to persist in proclaiming your word, in the power of Jesus Christ, Amen
           and honest, there was not a nasty word in his mind. He contributed an awful
```

The results of a search for "word" in the Collins CoBuild concordancer (extract).

Here the search term was 'word'. The concordancer searches through all the texts in its database for instances of the word "word" and then displays examples of sentences where "word" appears. The search term is shown in the middle, and a certain number of words from the original context are shown on either side. This type of concordancer (which is the most common) is known as Keyword-in-Context (KWIC).

If you wish to use a concordancer, you basically have two options. Either you can install a concordancer on your own PC as a standalone program, or you can use a web-based concordancer (which provides a similar service via a web page).

There are advantages to each approach. If you choose the first option, then you can decide exactly which texts you want to analyse. For example, you might want to collect samples of academic writing and analyse them to find useful collocations to teach your students. Another advantage is that you will not need to be online to use the concordancer. Also, standalone concordancers often have more features than web-based concordancers, allowing you to analyse texts in more detail (although you will probably not need all those features unless you are engaging in serious linguistic research).

However the main advantage of using a web-based concordancer like the Collins CoBuild or British National Corpus concordancers is the sheer size of the database which is analysed. According to Collins, their corpus contains more than 50 million words, while the BNC claim their corpus includes 100 million words. If you want to see how words are used in real English, then you will need to use one of these concordancers.

Let's take a look at some concordancers in more detail. We've chosen to concentrate on WordSmith Tools, Collins CoBuild, and the British National Corpus.

WordSmith Tools

WordSmith Tools is a standalone PC program developed by Mike Scott and sold by Oxford University Press. The package contains six tools which allow you to analyse texts – texts which you have to provide yourself.

The most useful tools are Concord (which creates concordances, finds collocates, and identifies common phrases), Wordlist (which generates word lists in alphabetical and frequency order), and Keywords (which identifies key words in a given text). The other three tools are utilities which allow you to view files, split up large files into smaller ones, and convert texts.

> **Tip**
> If you are looking for texts to use with a concordancer, try Project Gutenberg. Project Gutenberg is a website where you can download hundreds of e-texts – mainly out-of-copyright classics from authors like Dickens or the Brontes – in plain text format. It's an easy way to supply your concordancer with sample texts.

Using Standalone Software

WordSmith is an extremely powerful set of tools, and as such is used by professional lexicographers and linguists. Because of the sheer number of features, it can take a little while to learn how to use, and you will probably find you only need to use some of the features. However the help file is very useful and you can learn the basics fairly quickly.

At the time of writing, you can download a demo version of WordSmith (with limited functionality, naturally) for free from the OUP website. The price of a single user license is currently £51.95 (excl VAT). Buying a user license gives you a password which will unlock the complete functionality of your demo version.

Collins CoBuild

The Collins CoBuild Concordance and Collocation Sampler (to give it its full title) is a web-based concordancer, which is very popular with language teachers for one simple reason – it's free. Or rather, the demo version is free – you can also subscribe to the full service, but at £500 per year it's too expensive for the average teacher (although you might be able to persuade your institution to subscribe).

The 56 million word corpus is made up of texts from hundreds of sources, specially selected from Collins' 'Bank of English'. Ten million words of transcribed speech are included, from recordings made of real-life formal and informal speech situations. It also includes radio broadcasts, books (both fiction and non-fiction), newspapers and popular magazines, as well as a mass of more ephemeral material such as personal letters, advertisements, leaflets and brochures.

The sampler allows you to either make a concordance for a search term (or terms - you can also input phrases) or to find collocates for a particular word. An example of a concordance produced by the CoBuild sampler is shown in the illustration on page 122. In the demo version, if more than 40 instances of your search term are found, then only 40 lines selected from the total will be shown. You can choose to search in any or all of the following categories:

- British books, ephemera, radio, newspapers, magazines (containing 36m words);

- American books, ephemera and radio (10m words);
- British transcribed speech (10m words)

The collocation sampler shows which words occur most frequently with your search term. Again, in the demo version, if more than 100 collocations are found, then only the 100 statistically most important are shown. The collocation sampler also gives statistical information about the collocations found (which is probably of more interest to professional linguists than to the average language teacher).

British National Corpus

The British National Corpus (BNC) is a 100 million word collection of samples of written and spoken language from a wide range of sources, designed to represent a wide cross-section of current British English, both spoken and written. The project was carried out and is managed by an industrial/academic consortium led by Oxford University Press.

There are four main ways of accessing the BNC:

1. By obtaining a copy of the whole corpus for use on your own system. At the time of writing, this costs £250 (excluding VAT) for a full networked licence, or £50 (excluding VAT) for a single user licence. For this, you receive two CD-ROMs with the entire corpus.

2. By connecting to the British Library's Online BNC Service
This currently costs £60 per annum for one or two machines, £200 per annum for 3-10 machines or £500 per annum for 11-50 machines. To use the online service, you need to install a piece of software called SARA on your PC. This allows you to search the corpus and analyse your results.

3. By obtaining a copy of the BNC Sampler CD for use on your own computer system. The BNC Sampler CD-ROM contains a corpus with one million words of spoken text and one million words of written text, and software for processing it, including SARA and WordSmith Tools (described above). It currently costs £30.

10

Using Standalone Software

4. You can also do a 'simple search' of the BNC corpus, for free. This service is similar to the CoBuild Concordance Sampler - the main difference is that the BNC service returns whole sentences containing your search term (as opposed to the fixed number of words delivered by CoBuild). The illustration below shows the results of a search for 'word' in the BNC simple search option.

Results of your search

Your query was

```
word
```

Here is a random selection of 50 solutions from the 18739 found...

```
A6B 1727 Where My Word is unspoken.

ACN 931 In the beginning was the Word and The Word in
Dublin was Vibe.

AHA 976 It suffered so brutally from war and killing
that even after a second time around, in `;39, after the
havoc of Korea, the cut and thrust of Malaysia and Aden,
the carnage of the Falklands and the bizarre media-
encouraged sand-deaths in the Gulf —; even after all
that, the terrible word `;Gallipoli'; is burned deep
into the very fibre of every soul who was born in Bury,
or who had family there.

AHF 1201 The jubilant word from Kinnock's camp was that
Major was behaving more like an opposition leader than a
prime minister.

ARJ 2090 We are not Jewish, so where did I learn this
word?

B1J 1379 The Greek word eucharisto means to rejoice and
give thanks, so the Eucharist or communion is hardly a
time to be sad.

B7F 492 They are easy to read and spell for this word,
and variant pronunciations of `;banana'; are
recognisable across cultures.
```

Results of a search for "word" in the BNC "simple search" service (extract).

This demo version only delivers a maximum number of 50 hits (selected at random from the total). However this is generally enough for the purposes of the average language teacher.

Whether you choose to use the CoBuild demo service or the BNC demo will depend on what you want to do with the concordances. On the one hand, the CoBuild fixed length lines allow you to spot word patterns more easily. However the BNC whole sentence results give you a better idea of the context in which your chosen word occurs, although you have to find your focus word in the sentence by yourself - it's not highlighted.

Using a concordancer

There are two main ways to use a concordancer for language teaching, either outside class (to prepare a lesson or research a language question), or in class with students as a resource. Naturally the second option works best if you have internet access in class. However, if students don't have access to computers in the classroom, then you could also print out selected excerpts from the concordancer and give them everything on paper. If you take this approach, then you may want to edit the concordances produced – firstly, because a 40-line concordance takes up a lot of space, and secondly, to get rid of example sentences which are not relevant to your purposes.

How can you use a concordancer to answer language questions? Imagine you wanted to know the difference between 'proposal' and 'suggestion'. A dictionary may partly answer the question, but it will not necessarily show how the two words are used in real English. However, you could search for both in a concordancer and then compare the sentences in which both words are found, to make conclusions about which words collocate with "proposal" and "suggestion", and in which contexts each is liable to be found. Naturally you could also assign your students the same task, and let them work out the difference for themselves.

A variation on this technique is to produce a concordance for words which students do not know (you could perhaps select words which are likely to be unknown to students from a reading text you plan to use in class). Give the concordances to the students and get them to try to work out the meaning of the words from the examples. Generally this is easier when a student has several examples of a word used in context rather than just one.

Another activity is to get students to produce concordances for particular words and make a note of which words collocate with the target word. You could do this for example with common verbs like "get", "take", and "put" which can be used in very many different contexts. As mentioned above, the Collins CoBuild Sampler has a feature where you can search for the most common collocations for a particular word.

Concordancers can also be used for teaching grammar, specifically in awareness raising activities. For example, let's say you want to teach students how to use the word 'suggest'. You could give them example sentences such as:

He suggested going for a walk.

He suggested to go for a walk.

He suggested go for a walk.

He suggested that we go for a walk.

He suggested a walk.

Students then search for 'suggested' or 'he suggested' in the concordancer and deduce from the results which of the examples are acceptable English.

You could also make a worksheet with a variety of language questions (perhaps related to material you have recently covered in class) which the students can answer with the help of a concordancer. Here are some possible questions to include in a worksheet:

- What is the missing preposition in this sentence? "I can't rely … him".
- Which is correct – "make a party" or "give a party"?
- Correct the mistake in this sentence: "I'm looking forward to see you".
- Which adjectives often come before the word "location"?
- Which is more common – "keen student" or "enthusiastic student"?

If you show students how to use a freely-available concordancer (such as the Collins CoBuild or BNC demo versions) then you will have given them another tool to use to help them understand texts and learn vocabulary. A concordancer can be especially useful when used in combination with a good dictionary; the two resources complement each other.

Using a search engine as a concordancer

An alternative to using the concordancers described above is to use a search engine like Google as a concordancer. If you're familiar with concordancers, it may have occurred to you at some point that a search engine is in a sense like a concordancer, using the world's largest corpus – the internet. For example, if you search for the world 'goal' using a search engine, you will come up with thousands of sentences including the word 'goal'. Naturally it doesn't do the job quite as well as a tailor-made concordancer would – you will also get many headings and company names including the word goal, so a bit of sifting is called for to find good example sentences. On the other hand, the language on the internet is right up to date, unlike the language in a dictionary or a static corpus. The language on the internet is also anarchic, constantly-changing, full of obscenities and mistakes – all characteristics of 'real' language, unlike the sanitised English our students are likely to meet in English teaching course books.

So how can you exploit this with your students? Let's say your student wants to know the difference between 'target', 'aim', 'goal', and 'objective' (very hard to explain, as you may have experienced yourself). A conventional dictionary is unlikely to help very much. Instead, you could tell your student to search for each word in turn in a good search engine like Google, find ten (sensible) example sentences for each word, and copy and paste them into a word processor. Then the student can look at the different sentences and see if (s)he can distinguish any patterns. You could help by asking guiding questions such as "Are there any other words which occur with the key word?" or "In which contexts is this word typically used?".

> **Tip**
> If you are using the Collins CoBuild or BNC concordancers with young (or even not-so-young) students, be aware that its source texts consist of real English and hence contain words that might be considered offensive by some people.

Similarly, if a student wants to know which of 'for 10 years' and 'since ten years' is correct, ask the student to search for both phrases in a search engine and make a note of how many hits each alternative gets. The alternative with more hits is likely to be the correct one. This can be useful for students who need to write texts in English and want to check if a particular phrase is correct or not. Practically any common phrase will turn up in a search engine.

A word of caution – encourage the student to look carefully at the results which the search engine finds. If most of the results come from, say, Russian or Japanese websites, then the phrase is possibly not correct (assuming your definition of correct is 'acceptable to native speakers'). Similarly, the student should take the whole sentence into account. For example, few native speakers would say 'to make a party', but a search for 'to make a party' will yield many hits from websites written by native speakers. The reason is, the phrase 'to make a party' can occur in sentences such as 'How to make a party go with a bang' or 'Show your children how to make a party hat'. Despite this proviso, 'to have a party' yields substantially more hits than 'to make a party'. (Interestingly, 'to throw a party' comes up with even more, showing that this technique can also be useful to native speaker teachers wishing to know which variant is more common in real language.)

Naturally the suggestions for concordancer activities described above can also be adapted to work with a search engine used as a concordancer.

Audio recording software

As the name suggests, audio recording software allows you to record audio on your PC. You can also edit audio recordings – chopping them up, trimming them, getting rid of unwanted sections, or improving the sound quality. As audio recordings are obviously so important in language learning, knowing how to use an audio recording program can be extremely useful to a language teacher.

If you are using Windows, you probably have a piece of audio recording software already. It's called Sound Recorder and you should be able to find it at Start > Programs > Accessories > Entertainment > Sound Recorder. While Sound Recorder has the advantage of being free, the quality of the audio it produces leaves something to be desired. We use WaveLab from Steinberg, which gives much better results. It's not cheap, however—at the time of writing the full version costs EUR 548.99, while WaveLab Essential (which has fewer features) costs EUR 248.99. However cheaper shareware audio recorders are available. GoldWave is one popular shareware audio recorder - search for `audio recording software shareware' in a search engine to find more.

Audio recording software is particularly useful if you also have a CD burner on your PC. Basically this means you can record your own audio tracks and then burn them onto a CD, which you can then give to your students to listen to on any CD player for extra listening practice. Naturally you will need a microphone and a sound card in order to do this. The actual mechanics of how you do this will vary depending on your particular system - refer to your sound card and audio software instructions to find out what you need to do.

Here are some ideas for things to do with audio software and a CD burner.

- Get your English-speaking friends round to your house, and record them reading pre-written dialogues or engaging in spontaneous conversation. (If you're a fan of task-based learning, then you could record native speakers performing the same tasks that you ask your students to do.) Burn the recordings onto CD and use them in class.

- Record your students speaking, e.g. giving a presentation, taking part in a role-play, or discussing a topic. (If you don't have computer access in the classroom, then you will need a portable tape, MiniDisc, or digital voice recorder—you can transfer these audio recordings to your computer later.) Burn the recordings onto a CD to use in class, for example to give feedback, or to give to students at the end of the course so that they can hear how they have progressed.

- Record audio from the internet to use in class. (See below for details on how to do this.) Audio that you might want to record includes news stories, company presentations, songs, church sermons, radio programmes, and interviews.

10

Using Standalone Software

Recording audio from the internet

Imagine you've found the perfect audio news story on the BBC website to use with your class. "My pre-intermediate teenagers will love hearing about the trials and tribulations of Namibian coffee growers!" you think to yourself. There's only one problem – the audio is streamed so that you can only listen to it when connected to the BBC website. You don't have a computer in your classroom, so you want some way to record the audio so you can play it on a tape or CD to your charges. So you look at the options on your Real Player software. "That's funny," you think. "There's no 'record' option. But surely people want to record streaming audio so they can listen to it while offline?" Yes, but there's a simple reason why there's no record button. Remember that almost all the content you will listen to with streaming audio is copyright, and the copyright holders are understandably less than keen on you recording their copyright material.

Fortunately, there's a way around this. But before we get on to that, let us sternly state that neither we nor the publishers of this book condone the illegal recording and reproduction of copyright material. (But if all you're going to do is play it to your students once and then bin it, well, probably no-one's going to notice.)

Bearing that proviso in mind, here's how to do it. Actually there are two ways to do it – the low-tech way and the high-tech way. Let's look at the low tech way first. Basically this involves holding a cassette recorder near your computer speakers while the audio is streaming, and recording the audio that way. (We told you it was low tech.) This is certainly the quick and dirty way to do it, and if you have a good Internet connection, good speakers and a good cassette recorder, this may well give good enough results to use in class. A slightly more sophisticated way is to use a MiniDisc recorder, if you own one. You may be able to plug your MD recorder directly into your

> **Jargon box**
> Streaming audio is audio which is transmitted to your computer at the same time as you are listening to it. This has the advantage that you don't have to download a whole audio file (which tend to be big) before you listen to it.

sound card, and by pressing record on the recorder you can capture the audio directly on MD. (MD recorders give fantastic quality so if you're into recording stuff in general then you might want to invest in one, along with a good quality microphone.) Bear in mind though that the quality of your recording will never exceed the quality of the original – so if the audio is being streamed at 16 Kbps you're never going to get it to sound like CD quality, whatever you do.

Now let's look at the high tech way. This involves recording the streaming audio on to your hard disk, with the aid of audio recording software. For demonstration purposes we'll use Sound Recorder, which comes free with Windows. (If you're not using Windows, the principles should be the same.)

1. First of all, open Sound Recorder at its default location, which should be Start > Programs > Accessories > Entertainment > Sound Recorder.

2. Now open the Volume Control panel (it should be at Start > Programs > Accessories > Entertainment > Volume Control). You can also open it by right-clicking on the little loudspeaker icon in your system tray in the bottom right hand corner of your screen.

3. From the Options menu, select Properties. The Properties dialogue box appears. Under 'Adjust volume for' select Recording. New options will appear under "Show the following volume controls". Make sure that Wave is selected and click the OK button.

4. The Record Control dialogue box will appear. Check the box under Wave to select this as the recording source.

5. Now you're ready to start recording. Find the link to the audio file that you want to record, but don't click on it yet. Press the record button on Sound Recorder (the red circle) and quickly open the link. When the audio starts to stream you should be able to see a moving waveform on the Sound Recorder display.

6. If it only shows a straight line, that means it's not receiving any

Using Standalone Software

input. Check that you ticked the correct box in Record Control. (If you're not sure which box to check, select them one at a time in turn until you see a moving waveform in Sound Recorder.) Make sure that you're checking boxes in Record Control and not Play Control.

7. Once the audio segment you want to record has finished, press the stop button on Sound Recorder (the black square). Now you can press the play button and listen to the audio you have recorded. If you want to keep it then select Save from the File menu and save the file to your hard drive. Sound Recorder will save it as a .wav file.

8. Once you've saved your file on your computer, there are many things you can do with it. You could email it to someone as an attachment (but be warned – .wav files tend to be very big), you could save it on a floppy disk so you can play it on another computer, or you can burn it on a CD. Normally you can burn .wav files straight onto a CD and then listen to them on any CD player. Exactly how you burn it on a CD will depend on your CD burner software, but it should be straightforward (normally you have to find the .wav files in the source window in your CD recording software, then drag and drop them into the recording list).

Tip

If you want to include audio files on your website for people to listen to, or if you want to send audio files to students, then .wav files are probably too big (they will take too long to transfer over the internet, unless your extracts are very short). You will need to convert your .wav files into another format, making them smaller in the process. This will also reduce the quality of the recording, but if the recording only features voice then this will not matter - voice recordings are still understandable even if the audio is of low quality. Two popular formats are .wma from Microsoft (this plays in Windows Media Player, which comes free with Windows) and .rm (which can be listened to on RealPlayer, a free download from RealNetworks). If you wish to create files in these formats, you will need either Windows Media Encoder or Helix Producer, respectively. At the time of writing, you can download versions of each software for free—consult the <u>Windows Media</u> and <u>RealNetworks</u> websites for more information.

Office software

Most PCs running Windows have Microsoft Office (or an equivalent suite of programs, such as Microsoft Works) installed on them. Here are some ideas for using Office software in your teaching.

Word processor

Obviously a word processor like Microsoft Word is enormously useful for a language teacher wishing to produce his or her own worksheets. Here are some tips for producing exercises with a minimum of effort.

- Use the 'search and replace' function (found in the 'edit' menu) to change all the vowels in a text to asterisks. Students have to recreate the text by working out what the missing vowels are.
- Use 'search and replace' to remove all the spaces in a text (to do this, type a space in the 'search' box but leave the 'replace' box empty). Students have to separate the words.
- Select the whole text and change the font to Wingdings (or another font which consists solely of symbols). Students have to crack the code by working out which symbol stands for which letter. Give them a couple of letters to get them started.

> **Tip**
> Notepad is a simple text editor which comes as standard with every version of Windows. (Normally you can find it under Start>Programs>Accessories.) It can be very useful if you are making worksheets using material from web pages. You may have noticed that if you copy and paste a section of text directly from a web page into Word, it can take a long time for Word to carry out the operation, and you are often left with a lot of unwanted images and formatting (such as tables) in your document. To avoid this, copy the text from the web page first into Notepad (which removes all the images and formatting from the text) and then copy the plain text from Notepad into Word.

Students can also use a word processor to help them write English correspondence. Students can write their text in Word and use the spellcheck function to find spelling mistakes. Even if their version of Word is in another language, they can generally change the language to English to spell check a document, which many students do not realise. This can be especially useful if students are using an email program which doesn't have a spellcheck function. They can write their text in Word, check the spelling, then copy and paste it into their email program before sending the email.

Spreadsheets

You might think a spreadsheet like Microsoft Excel would be an unlikely candidate for language teaching. However it can be useful for students to make a record of vocabulary items they have encountered. For example, students can write English words in the first column, with their definitions or translations in the second column. Example sentences could go in the third column. One advantage of a spreadsheet is that lists can be sorted alphabetically with the click of a mouse.

If you're not into the idea of alphabetically-sorted vocabulary lists, then you can ask students to organise vocabulary into, for example, different lexical areas. Each lexical area could be given a separate table within the spreadsheet. Alternatively you might have a verb in the first column and a noun which collocates with the verb in the second column.

Students can learn their vocabulary with the spreadsheet in the same way that they might work with record cards. Resize the spreadsheet window so that it is the size of one spreadsheet cell. Use the arrow keys or mouse to move to a cell with a vocabulary item you want the student to revise. The student must then define or translate the word. Their answer can be checked by simply moving one column to the right, where the definition or translation is contained. Alternatively, show the student the second column and ask them to produce the target word.

Students can work with their vocabulary spreadsheets alone, with you simply checking them intermittently for mistakes or for revision purposes. Or you can work with the spreadsheets in class – this can be practical if you are teaching in an institution or company where students have ready access to computers. If you are teaching a group and the students have access to the same computer, or the same directory on a network, then two or more people can work on the same spreadsheet, adding vocabulary items as they learn them. This way students can pool their knowledge and help each other. It can also be motivating for students to watch the spreadsheet grow and see how many vocabulary items they have covered in the course.

It is also possible to use Excel to make interactive multiple-choice exercises, similar to those which can be produced using HTML and JavaScript. You can do this using macros within Excel (how to do this is unfortunately outside the scope of this book - refer to the Excel help function for more information). However, unless you are already familiar with macros, it is probably easier to make the exercises as web pages – the end result is very similar and web pages give you more flexibility.

Presentation software

Presentation software packages like PowerPoint from Microsoft allow you to make slides to accompany a presentation. If your students have to make presentations as part of their daily work, then they probably already have PowerPoint presentations in English. Naturally you can get them to give these presentations to you in class for practice.

> **Tip**
> Microsoft Office normally comes with templates for different kinds of business documents. You can find them by going to Start > New Office Document or by selecting New from the File menu in any of the Office applications. These templates include things like sample business letters, résumés, business plan presentations and so on. These are ideal for using in class if you want to teach students how to do any of these things — simply tell students which template to use and then get them to add their own content. Even if the version of Windows you are using isn't in English, the templates can still be useful, as they explain to students in their own language what content they should provide. They could also be useful for a discussion about how, say, résumés in the students' language differ from English résumés.

Using Standalone Software

You can also get students to use PowerPoint in class to prepare and give presentations. Even if students never have to give presentations in real life, this is still good language practice. Here are some possible ideas for student presentations:

- places to visit in the student's home town;
- a short history of the student's country;
- a student's future career plans;
- a student's hobby or interest (eg a favourite music group).

There are also many readymade PowerPoint presentations on the internet that you can use with your students. Simply do a search for .ppt in Google to find a selection (.ppt is the file extension for PowerPoint files). Add keywords to focus your search. For example, if you wanted to find marketing presentations, you could search for 'marketing .ppt'.

Once you've found some useful presentations, you can save them to your hard drive by choosing File > Save as. Then you can use them in class, either in electronic format if you have access to computers in the classroom, or on paper if you print the presentation out. Make sure you give students plenty of time to read through the presentation and practise before asking them to give their presentation to the class.

> **Tip**
> If you're teaching English in a company, look for presentations from their competitors—students are always fascinated by what the competition is up to.

Conclusion

Standalone software can be of great use to you;

- if you and/or your students are already familiar with a certain software package;
- if you and the students don't have access to computers in the classroom, but do in another place;
- by keeping recurring costs low, such as online time (once the software has been bought it can be used indefinitely with no extra costs);
- as it may allow you to exchange materials with other teachers – Word files for instance, .ppt documents etc.

Chapter 11

Blogs

'Blogs' – you may well have heard of them and you may even know that blog is short for weblog, but do you know what they actually are and how you can use them for teaching and learning? Hopefully by the end of this chapter you'll be able to answer 'yes' to both of those questions!

Blogs are somewhat controversial. Some people love them, while others just don't quite see the point – for reasons we will see below.

In its most basic form, a blog is an online diary. Blogs were originally used by people who didn't have much, if any, knowledge of HTML, FTP and all that sort of thing, but who wanted to put up some content onto a website. Sites such as Blogger and eBloggy came about which allow users to register (for free, or a small fee), then type some text into a chosen template, and with one click make that text available on the web for the world to see. The blog owner can then log into their blog however often they like, making changes to text they've already written, and add new text. Each user's blog has its own unique URL which the author can distribute, just like a website address, which others can then visit. In addition to text, many blogs now allow additional content such as images, links and audio/video-clips, as well as giving the user more control over the navigation and general look and feel of their blog, thereby basically allowing the user to create their own fully-featured website.

Blogs: yes or no?

Proponents of blogs praise the ease with which they allow 'low-tech' users to build an internet presence, while others say that building and publishing your own site using tools such as FrontPage or Dreamweaver is so easy now that using a blog isn't really necessary. Others think that blogs make it far too easy for just anyone to post their thoughts onto the web when nobody's really interested, but that's another story!

Because it's so easy to set up a blog, the blogging community is growing day by day. Many blogs out there contain little more than "Hi, this is my blog!" while others are very rich in content, have specific focuses or are very well-written and entertaining.

Things to do with a blog

So why have a blog? Well, there's a range of things you and/or your students can use blogs for:

- If you enjoy writing for writing's sake, you can post your daily thoughts and observations on a blog for your students to read. This is a nice way to complement an extensive group class, for example. You can set them tasks either in class, by email or on the blog itself to help them practise their reading and comprehension skills.

- You can structure a blog by category, adding relevant content in each one. This may include a collection of links for students to explore, reading exercises, and more.

- You could put images or drawings on your blog to help students develop their writing skills. For example, students could be encouraged to choose a different image each week, write a description, and email it to you and/or the other students, or bring it in to class. Especially if you are preparing students for certain exams, this will help them with directly relevant skills.

11

Blogs

- Your students could set up blogs for themselves – for example, to post their descriptions of the images from the previous exercise. Alternately, they can use it to post a diary of their life overseas (if they're studying English in a foreign country, for example), to keep a diary in order to practise their writing skills, or to work on exercises collaboratively if they are taking part in a distance online course.
- Students can use blogs to write feature-length articles/essays about a topic of their own interest, then publicise the URL on discussion forums or email lists used by people with similar interests. This is likely to yield feedback from 'real', native speakers (as opposed to a teacher), which is likely to be very satisfying for your students.

These are just some ideas of how blogs can be used. Because a blog is for many intents and purposes a form of website, just about any exercise-type you can think of for websites can also be used for blogs, but perhaps more easily.

Conclusion

In conclusion, a blog is for you if you:

- want to be able to post thoughts and ideas to the web with very little or no technical knowledge;
- enjoy writing and like the idea that anyone out there can read what you have written;
- want to set your students tasks or exercises on the web without setting up your own fully-fledged website;
- want your students to have their own online presence without spending a lot of time training them in how to build a website.

Appendix 1

Website addresses

Introduction
www.modernenglishpublishing.com

Chapter 1 Using Email

Hotmail Free email provider
www.hotmail.com

Yahoo Free email provider
www.yahoo.com

Email discussion groups
http://groups.yahoo.com

FAU Netiquette (Arlene Rinaldo's The Net: User Guidelines and Netiquette)
www.fau.edu/netiquette/net/dis.html

Chapter 2 Using Websites for Language Teaching

Search engines
www.google.com
www.yahoo.com
www.altavista.com

EFL websites

Dave Sperling's ESL Café
www.eslcafe.com

Free interactive, multimedia resources for learners and teachers of English
www.e-mesh.com

This site is for people who have either started a career in teaching English as a foreign or second language, or who want to start one.
www.eflweb.com

Free resources for language learners and teachers
www.englishclub.com

Listening exercises for learners of English
www.englishlistening.com

The History Channel
www.historychannel.com

The History Channel UK
www.thehistorychannel.co.uk

This Day in History (on the History Channel website)
www.historychannel.com/tdih

Hello!
www.hellomagazine.com

BBC's Music Profiles
www.bbc.co.uk/music/profiles

A - Z lyrics
www.azlyrics.com

BBC
www.bbc.co.uk

CNN
www.cnn.com

The Guardian
www.guardian.co.uk

The Times
www.timesonline.co.uk

Appendix 1

Internet Movie Database
www.imdb.com

Astrology.com
www.astrology.com

Calorie Control Council
www.caloriecontrol.org

This Day in Rock & Roll History
www.arrowfm.com/cgi/history.pl

BBC Sports
http://news.bbc.co.uk/sport

Soccernet
http://soccernet.espn.go.com

The Guardian's Football pages
http://football.guardian.co.uk

The Central Directory for English Soccer on the Net
www.e-soccer.com

DatingDirect
www.datingdirect.com

Totaljobs
www.totaljobs.com

Weather.com, international weather reports
(**www.weather.com/common/welcomepage/world.html?from=globalnav** is the direct URL for international weather reports)
www.weather.com

Biography.com
www.biography.com

How Stuff Works
www.howstuffworks.com

The All Movie Guide
www.allmovie.com

Appendix 1

Chapter 3 WebQuests

Bernie Dodge's Webquest site
http://webquest.org

Chapter 5 - Text-chat and Instant Messaging

Yahoo! Chat
http://chat.yahoo.com

Vance Steven's Webheads
www.geocities.com/vance_stevens/papers/evonline2002/webheads.htm

mIRC download site
www.mirc.com

AOL Instant Messenger
www.aim.com

Yahoo! Messenger
http://messenger.yahoo.com

ICQ
www.icq.com

MSN Messenger
http://messenger.msn.com

Jabber
www.jabber.com

Trillian
www.ceruleanstudios.com

PayPal
www.paypal.com

Chapter 6 - Using Internet Audio/video-conferencing

PalTalk
www.paltalk.com

Microsoft NetMeeting
www.microsoft.com/windows/netmeeting

Appendix 1

NetMeeting HQ list of ILS servers
www.netmeetinghq.com/ils/servers.phtml

Meeting by Wire website with detailed information about NetMeeting
www.meetingbywire.com

Chapter 7 - Learning Management Systems

Blackboard
www.blackboard.com

WebCT
www.webct.com

Virtual-U by Virtual Learning Environments Inc
www.vlei.com/products.htm

Chapter 8 – Creating your own website

Microsoft FrontPage
http://office.microsoft.com/home/

Macromedia Dreamweaver
www.macromedia.com/software/dreamweaver/

Adobe GoLive
www.adobe.com/products/golive/main.html

Amaya
www.w3.org/Amaya/

Evrsoft 1st Page 2000
www.evrsoft.com/1stpage2.shtml

Wrox publishers
www.wrox.com

O'Reilly publishers
www.oreilly.com

Writing HTML, by the Maricopa Center for Learning & Instruction
www.mcli.dist.maricopa.edu/tut

Hot Potatoes
web.uvic.ca/hrd/halfbaked/index.htm

WebTeacher JavaScript tutorial
www.webteacher.com/javascript/

PageResource.com JavaScript tutorial
www.pageresource.com/jscript/

W3schools.com JavaScript tutorial
www.w3schools.com/js/default.asp

Macromedia Flash
www.macromedia.com/software/flash

Lycos
www.lycos.com

Yahoo
www.yahoo.com

Tripod webhosting
www.tripod.lycos.com

Geocities webhosting
geocities.yahoo.com/home

Webmonkey – tutorials and more
webmonkey.wired.com/webmonkey/

CuteFTP
www.globalscape.com/cuteftp/

WS_FTP
www.ipswitch.com/downloads/index.html

InterNIC
www.internic.com

Uwhois (Universal Who Is)
www.uwhois.com

ICANN - Internet Corporation for Assigned Names and Numbers
www.icann.com

IANNA – Internet Assigned Numbers Authority
www.ianna.com

DENIC
www.denic.de

Appendix 1

Chapter 9 - Authoring Software: Interactive Exercises

Hot Potatoes
http://web.uvic.ca/hrd/halfbaked

Quia
www.quia.com

The Discovery Channel Quiz Center
http://school.discovery.com/quizcenter/quizcenter.html

The Easy Test Maker
www.easytestmaker.com

Chapter 10 - Standalone Software

Collins CoBuild Concordancer
http://titania.cobuild.collins.co.uk/form.html

British National Corpus Concordancer
http://thetis.bl.uk/lookup.html

Oxford University Press
www.oup.com

Project Gutenberg
www.gutenberg.org

Steinberg, makers of WaveLab
www.steinberg.net

GoldWave
www.goldwave.com

Windows Media
www.microsoft.com/windows/windowsmedia

RealProducer/Helix Producer
www.realnetworks.com/products/producer/index.html

Chapter 11 - Blogs

Blogger
www.blogger.com

eBloggy
www.ebloggy.com
www-writing.berkeley.edu/tesl-ej/ej22/int.html

"The Bloglog is a directory of English teaching and travel related diaries, journals and weblogs worldwide"
www.tesall.com/bloglog.html

A blog by a teacher containing teaching ideas
http://realbooks.blogspot.com/

Appendix 2

Language-learning CD-ROMs

General English

Active Listening in English Friend, Don. (Sky Software House, 2002)

Beat the Clock (Educational Software Products, 1999)

Citizen of the World (Edulang, 1998)

Click into English (Clarity)

Crossword Challenge (Educational Software Products, 1999)

Exterminator! (Educational Software Products, 2003)

Focus on Grammar CD-ROM Schoenberg, Irene E. et al. (Longman, 1998)

Gramster: New Edition. Brett, Paul. (Edulang)

Issues in English Kaufmann, Heather. (Protea Textware, 1996)

Let's Go Interactive (OUP)

Listen and Learn English: Starters, Movers and Flyers (Delta Publishing, 2004)

Longman English Interactive Rost, Michael & Fuchs, Marjorie. (Longman, 2003)

MindGame Rinvolucri, Mario. (Clarity, 1999)

Murder Mystery Friend, Don. (Sky Software House, 1999)

Read It! (Clarity)

Read Up-Speed Up Friend, Don. (Sky Software House, 2001)

Reward CD-ROM (Macmillan, 1999)

Snapshot (Longman, 2001)

Storyboard (Wida/Eurocentres)

Technology in Context Hill, Peter et al. (World Language Productions, 2002)

Tense Buster New Edition. (Clarity)

Testmaster Jones, Christopher. (Wida/Eurocentres)

Textris (Educational Software Products, 2003)

The Grammar CD-ROM Freebairn, I & Rees-Parnall, H. (Longman)

Vocabster (Edulang, 2002)

VOX Pop: Learn to express your opinions in English (Lingonet)

Pronunciation

Phonemic Alphabet in English (Sky Software House)

Similar Sounds Don Friend. (Sky Software House, 1999)

Stress and Rhythm (Sky Software House)

Word and Phrasal Stress (Sky Software House)

Business English

Business Connections O'Driscoll, Nina et al. (Longman, 2003)

Business Territory 1: Business English. (Lingonet, 1997)

Business To Go. Falla, Tim. (Macmillan, 1997)

English For Business. (Edulang, 1996)

English for Telephoning CD-ROM. Stirling, Johanna. (Delta Publishing, 2004)

Letter Writer: Letters, Faxes and Emails. (Clarity, 1998)

Multilevel Business English Programme CD-ROM. (PH)

Talking Business. Brieger, Nick & Comfort, Jeremy. (Longman, 2003)

Telephoning in English CD-ROM. Revell, Rod & Naterop, B. Jean. (CUP, 1999)

The Language of Meetings. (Abacus, 2000)

The Language of Negotiating. (Abacus, 1997)

The Language of Presentations. (Abacus, 2000)

The Language of Telephoning. (Abacus, 1999)

English for Academic Purposes

Read It! (Clarity, 1997)

Study Skills Success. (Clarity, 2002)

The Report Writer. (Clarity)

Exam Preparation

CAE Tutor. (Educational Software Products, 1999)

CPE Tutor. (Educational Software Products, 1999)

FCE Grammar ROM. Freebairn, Ingrid & Rees-Parnall, Hilary. (Longman, 2000)

FCE Tutor. (Educational Software Products, 1999)

First Certificate Gold Interactive. Acklam, Richard & Burgess, Sally. (Longman, 2003)

The First Certificate Creative Writing CD-ROM. Chadwick, Steve. (CUP, 1999)

TOEIC Preparation Interactive. Lougheed, Lin. (Longman, 2003)

Reference works

Collins Cobuild on CD-ROM. (HarperCollins, 2003)

Dictionary of Banking & Finance - Electronic Dictionary. (Bloomsbury, 1999)

English Dictionary for Students. (Bloomsbury, 1999)

Longman Interactive American English Dictionary. (Longman, 1997)

Longman Interactive English Dictionary: New edition. (Longman, 2000)

Oxford Advanced Learner's Dictionary CD-ROM. (OUP, 2000)

Appendix 3

Books

Barrett, Barney & Sharma, Pete: **The Internet and Business English.** (Summertown Publishing, 2003)

Crystal, David: **Language and the Internet.** (CUP, 2001)

Dudeney, Gavin: **The Internet and the Language Classroom: A practical guide for teachers.** (CUP, 2000)

Lewis, Gordon: **The Internet and Young Learners**. Series Editor: Alan Maley. (OUP, 2004)

Sharma, Pete: **CD-ROM: A Teacher's Handbook.** (Summertown Publishing, 1998)

Sperling, Dave: **Dave Sperling's Internet Activity Workbook**. (Prentice Hall, 1999)

Teeler, Dede & Gray, Peta: **How to Use the Internet in ELT.** (Longman, 2000)

Windeatt, Scott; Hardisty, David; and Eastment, David: **The Internet**. Series Editor: Alan Maley. (OUP, 2000)

Appendix 4

Appendix 4

Keyboard shortcuts

Toggling between windows
If you have several windows open at the same time, you can 'toggle' between them (switch from one to another) by holding down the Alt key on your keyboard and then pressing the tab button while keeping the Alt key pressed down. You will see icons representing each of the windows which are currently open; keep pressing the tab key until the window is highlighted that you want to use. Release the tab and Alt keys and that window will open. With a bit of practice this will become a much quicker way of opening a window than using your mouse.

Highlight a word
Ctrl + Shift + left/right arrow

Highlight a paragraph
Go to beginning/end of paragraph, then Ctrl + Shift + up/down arrow

Highlight entire document
Ctrl + A

Cut
Highlight word first, then Ctrl +X

Paste
Ctrl + v

Copy
Highlight word first, then Ctrl + C

Undo
Ctrl + Z

Jump to end of word
Ctrl + left/right arrow

Jump to end of paragraph
Ctrl + down arrow

Tab
When working with a form on a website, use the tab key to jump from one field to another
Redo an 'undone' operation
Ctrl + Y

Find
Ctrl + F

Save a file
Ctrl + S

Open a file
Ctrl + O

Print
Ctrl + P

Put highlighted word(s) into bold (Microsoft Word)
Ctrl + B

Put highlighted word(s) into italics (Microsoft Word)
Ctrl + I

Underline highlighted word(s) (Microsoft Word)
Ctrl + U

Glossary

A

Adobe Acrobat® Software program which allows a user to create a PDF document containing text, images, illustrations and more. Viewers of the PDF document need the free Acrobat Reader (downloadable from www.adobe.com) to read it. An advantage of using PDF format is that the document looks identical on all computers, unlike some documents produce in Microsoft Word, for example.

alias A name or identification that is not one's real name. Used when logging into a chat room, for example.

Application Service Provider (ASP) A company which allows use of particular software while online. The user therefore does not need to download and install the software on their own computer. The company may charge the user on a per-use basis, monthly, or in some other form. Advantages of an ASP model are that the software is always up-to-date, the user doesn't need to download and install large amounts of software, and infrequent users are likely to pay less than if they had to buy the entire software bundle.

asynchronous Not at the same time. An asynchronous message is one written by one user, and read by another user at a different time. Examples of asynchronous messages are emails, and messages written on discussion forums. See also *synchronous*.

attachment A file attached to an email and sent along as a separate document. If a user has a text file (e.g. a Microsoft Word file) already saved on their computer, for example, (s)he can attach it to an email and send it in that way, rather than copying the text into an email.

audio file A file containing sound (e.g. a voice recording or music)

authoring software Programs used to create (as opposed to read/play back) documents or files. Some programs have both authoring and display capabilities (e.g. Microsoft Word) while others can only create or only play back content. Often used within ELT to refer to programs such as Hot Potatoes which can be used to create interactive exercises.

B

bandwidth Within the context of the internet, bandwidth refers to the internet connection speed available to a user. See also *broadband* and *dialup connection*.

blended learning/blended solution A model which combines some face-to-face teaching with online learning.

blog Short for weblog. A website which is created using web-based software. Blogs are often used as online journals or news resources. They tend to be easy to set up and maintain, allowing the blog author to post regular updates.

broadband An internet connection faster than a dialup connection (maximum 56.6kbps) or ISDN (128kbps). Examples of broadband connections are ADSL, cable or satellite.

browser A program that allows a user to view websites. Examples of common browsers are Internet Explorer, Netscape Navigator, Firefox and Opera.

buddy A friend or acquaintance which whom a user regularly communicates online using an *Instant Messaging* program.

button An image on a website or CD-ROM which a user clicks on to make something happen. Buttons are often used to link to other pages within a website or for submitting online forms, for example.

C

CD burner A device capable of creating a CD. CD burners can be internal (i.e. built into a computer) or external (i.e. attached to a computer via a cable). Most CD burners can also play back CDs.

CD-ROM A disk identical in appearance to a music CD which contains data of any kind. This may include text, animations, videos, images or music.

channel When logging into an *Internet Relay Chat* (IRC) various channels are available. Each channel allows a user to communicate live with other people who have also chosen that particular channel.

chat A mechanism which allows online users (usually in different geographical areas) to communicate with each other live via text (though some chat mechanisms now also support audio).

chat client A program installed on a user's computer that allows the user to take part in an online *chat*.

chat room A web-based program that allows users in different geographical locations to take part in an online *chat*. Users logged into a chat room do not however need a *chat client* installed on their computer.

concordancer A program that creates a list of the principle words used within a particular text or collection of texts (e.g. books or articles). Such a concordance may then be used to gather information about frequency of specific words or how they are used in language e.g. which other words they collocate with.

connectivity The type, quality or reliability of a user's online connection

Content Management System (CMS) A facility which allows the storing and organisation of digital content. This may also include mechanisms that allow collaborative work on the content. Many current websites can be edited online using a CMS.

context menu A menu which offers a user different options depending on the current context. For example, a website may have different menus on different sub-areas of the site, offering the user options specific to that sub-area. Similarly, right-clicking (i.e. clicking the right button of a computer mouse) in a program will normally open a context menu, offering the user different choices depending on the program currently being used or the work currently being done.

copy and paste Copying text or other content from one area of a document to another one (or from one document to a different one). The first step is to select/highlight the content to be copied, then use the Copy command in the current program (often found under the Edit menu, or by holding down the

Ctrl button and pressing C once) to copy the content. The next step is to place the cursor in the area into which the content is to be copied (either in the same document or another one), then choosing the Paste command (again either under Edit, or by doing Ctrl and V).

course management system A facility which allows the administration of an online course. This usually comprises student management (enrolment; storing of grades; registration to individual courses etc) and may also combine content management (see **Content Management System**).

D

data transfer rates The speed at which data is sent/received on a network e.g. when connected to the Internet.

database A set of information, stored electronically and usually structured in a specific way for a specific purpose. Most databases can be searched according to certain criteria, new information can be entered and existing information can be viewed or exported in such a way as to be useful for other purposes (such as creating a mailing list from a database containing e.g. customer information).

dedicated videoconferencing Videoconferencing using equipment whose only function is to be used for videoconferencing and which cannot be used for any other purposes.

desktop The view on a computer screen when no programs are open. The desktop usually shows a number of icons, allowing the user to start various programs. The desktop is also a convenient place for the user to (temporarily) save documents or files, as they are easily accessible.

DHTML Dynamic HTML. An extension of HTML which allows greater interaction between a user and the web page, often however at the expense of compatibility with different browsers.

dialog box A window that appears prompting the user for action. A dialog box may ask for confirmation (e.g. "Are you sure you want to delete this file?") or ask the user to make a particular choice. A dialog box usually appears when the user has initiated a particular procedure which needs further clarification.

dialup connection An internet connection established via a dialup modem and through the regular telephone system. A dialup connection has a maximum connection speed of 56.6kpbs.

directory Another name for a *folder*. Also used within Microsoft NetMetting to mean a mechanism to which online users of Microsoft NetMeeting can log on in order to make themselves available for NetMeeting calls by others.

discussion forum A web-based system that allows users to write messages which stay on the forum permanently, or until actively removed. Other users can read previously posted messages and reply. Discussion forums are often organised around specific themes.

domain name A unique, registered combination of letters and numbers which can be used to identify websites or email addresses. Domain names consist of two parts - a letter/number combination, followed by a dot and a suffix such as com or co.uk .In the website address www.microsoft.com for example the domain name is microsoft.com

download To copy a file from the internet or an intranet onto a local computer.

drag and drop To move an on-screen object such as a piece of text or an image from one location to another one by clicking on the object with the mouse, 'dragging' it to the new location by moving the mouse, and then 'dropping' it by releasing the mouse button.

drop box A web-based mechanism that allows students to deposit files for a teacher/marker. A drop box is usually one component of a *Virtual Learning Environment*, though free-standing drop boxes are also available.

drop-down menu A kind of *menu* usually found in programs or websites. Drop-down menus allow a user to choose one of multiple selections which appear when clicking a down-arrow symbol or placing the mouse cursor over the menu name.

DVD Digital Versatile Disc. A silver disc, similar in appearance to a CD-ROM, but which can hold substantially more data. A DVD can hold video, images, text and more.

E

E-learning Short for electronic learning. A term which can encompass any form of learning which makes use of electronic devices or media whether it is in a face-to-face scenario or by distance.

email (also written e-mail) Short for electronic mail. A system which allows one internet user to send a message and/or files to one or more other users.

email account An account set up with an email provider, or set up for a user by an employer for example, that allows a user to send and receive email.

email address A unique address which allows a user to receive emails. An email address consists of three parts: a letter/number combination (e.g. eric39) followed by the @ symbol followed by a domain name.

email discussion group An email distribution system which connects a number of email users. Members of an email discussion group are usually like-minded people who exchange information and opinions on a certain topic. An individual user subscribes to an email discussion group (usually free of charge) and is then able to send an email to the discussion group's unique email address. The email is then distributed automatically to all members of the discussion group, who can then in turn reply to the email.

e-text (also e-book) A book in electronic format which can be read on a computer, PDA or other similar device.

extension A code (usually three letters) following a filename that indicates to a user and to the computer what type of file it is, e.g. a file extension .doc signals that the file is a Microsoft Word document, while the extension .pdf signals that it is an Adobe Acrobat Portable Document Format file.

F

face-to-face (F2F) In person, not by distance (often contrasted with e-learning). A F2F lesson is one where the teacher and the students are in the same room together.

file sharing A mechanism which allows multiple users on different computers to work on the same file together, at the same time. Most internet conferencing tools contain such a feature.

Glossary

file transfer A process whereby a file is transferred from one user or server to another one.

firewall A computer or network protection mechanism, often used by companies but also individuals to protect their computers from hackers and viruses.

Flash A file format developed by Macromedia. Flash files (or 'animations') can allow for interactivity between the user and the file, e.g. a user may click part of the animation in order to trigger a certain event. Many current websites use Flash for animations, advertising, or games. Within ELT, Flash can be used to create interactive exercises.

folder A filing device on a computer that allows a user to group files in a way that is meaningful to them. Often depicted with a 'folder' icon e.g. on the desktop.

font A typeface or style. Common fonts include Times New Roman and Arial.

frames A web page may consist of multiple frames such as a left-hand navigation frame and a main frame. If a page consists of multiple frames, each page within the frames is separate, though they are usually linked. It is often possible to scroll each page in the separate frame up or down independently of the other one(s).

freeware - Software that can be used free of charge. See also *shareware*.

FTP - File Transfer Protocol. See *file transfer*.

H

hard copy A printed version of an electronic document.

hard drive A storage device which is permanently fixed within a computer and where the operating system, programs and data are stored.

headset A device consisting of earphones and microphone which a user can wear on their head (e.g. for online audio-conferencing)

HTML Hypertext Markup Language. The computer language in which web pages are written.

hyperlink A piece of text or an image within one web page which, when clicked, takes the user to another page or subsection of a page.

I

icon An image representing something such as a program installed on a computer. Clicking (or double-clicking) an icon starts up the program it represents.

Information Technology (IT) The field of study and work dealing with technology such as computers and telecommunications.

input box A field in an online information-gathering form into which a user can type text.

installation The process of putting a program onto a computer in order to be able to use it. In order to install a program, an installation file is needed which can usually either be downloaded from the software manufacturer's website, or copied from a CD-ROM etc.

Instant Messaging (IM) Communicating live online (usually via instant text messages) with another user using a specialised program. Examples of IM programs are Microsoft Messenger, Yahoo! Messenger, ICQ and AOL IM.

interactive exercise An exercise which reacts to an action performed by a user. Most interactive exercises allow the user to click on specified areas or choose options in some other way, then display something as a result of the user's actions. Within ELT, interactive exercises can be used for e.g. grammar or vocabulary multiple-choice or gap-fill exercises.

interface 1) The visual display ("user interface" or "graphical user interface" (GUI)) the user sees on the screen which allows the user to input information or otherwise interact with the computer software. 2) An electronic component used to connect computer devices together e.g. a USB interface.

internet (also written Internet) An international network of computers. The internet enables users to display and visit websites, send and receive emails, transfer files and more.

internet conferencing Communicating live online with other users, usually incorporating audio, video and file-sharing capabilities.

Glossary

Internet Locator Service A system which allows users of certain internet conferencing tools (e.g. Microsoft NetMeeting, CU-See-Me) to make themselves known to other users. Once logged on to an ILS, users can select each other and establish an online conference.

internet presence A company or individual is said to have an online or internet presence if they have their own website or feature on another website (such as that of an agent's).

Internet Relay Chat (IRC) One of the original chat-systems on the internet, IRC allows users to log on and communicate with each other live via text. In order to take part in IRC a user needs an IRC client (a program specifically designed for IRC). IRC has been largely superseded by <I>*Instant Messaging*.

IP address A number uniquely identifying a computer while connected to the internet. Some computers, such as computers attached to a corporate network, have static IP addresses, i.e. their IP addresses are always the same. Others, in particular home computers which connect to the internet via an Internet Service Provider, have dynamic IP addresses, i.e. they are assigned a different IP address every time they log on to the internet.

ISDN (Integrated Services Digital Network) A type of digital connection established by cables which allow transfer speeds of 64kbps or multiples thereof. ISDN can be used for dedicated videoconferencing, internet connections and more.

ISP (Internet Service Provider) A company which enables internet access to individual users or companies, usually for a fee of some sort.

J

Java A programming language. Often used within ELT for exercises, games and applications. Java applications may be embedded in web pages but can also be distributed on CD-ROM or by other means.

JavaScript A coding language which can be embedded in HTML in order to extend the functionality of a web page. Different from *Java,* which is a programming language in its own right and separate from HTML.

K

Kbps Kilobytes per second. A measure of data-transfer.

keyboard shortcut A combination of keyboard keys which, when pressed simultaneously, have the same effect as certain mouse commands. For example, within Microsoft Windows, holding down the Ctrl key and pressing C at the same time has the same effect as clicking the Copy button.

kilobyte A measure of data (1 kilobyte - 1000 bytes).

L

lag Delay in communication which is introduced by the network. Usually used in the context of Internet Relay Chat.

learning platform A wide-ranging term applied to any computer-based system that contains content and/or a management system for the purpose of delivering or managing learning.

link rot The phenomenon where links on a website gradually become outdated.

log on/off To connect/disconnect to a closed system such as a network, the internet, or an email program.

look and feel The visual appearance of a program or environment.

lurk To receive and read messages without replying or participating in a discussion. A user may choose to lurk on an email discussion group for instance, reading the conversations that are taking place but not actively contributing. Lurking is a good idea for discussion group <I>*newbies*.

M

macro A pre-programmed sequence of actions or events that can be started by a user. For example, it is possible to create a macro in Microsoft Word that performs a specific sequence of mouse-clicks or actions. This can be useful when the same actions are performed repeatedly e.g. searching for and replacing certain words.

megabytes A measure of data (1 megabyte = 1000 kilobytes)

menu A list of options within a program or website. The user chooses the desired option by clicking on it with the mouse or pressing a certain key.

moderate To control messages that are sent to a particular forum such as a chat room or an email discussion list. A moderator may set up a forum in such a way that any messages sent must first be sanctioned by the moderator before they are released to all other participants. A forum may be moderated for a number of reasons such as the filtering of obscenities or for keeping a discussion focused on a particular topic.

multimedia Containing or consisting of more than one medium, e.g. text and sound, sound and vision etc.

multiway In the context of internet audio conferencing, a multiway system is one that allows more than two participants to hear and speak to one another in an online audio conference.

N

netiquette The rules - stated or otherwise - of online communication. While there are a number of guidelines that are generally accepted by internet users, some usergroups set up their own netiquette by which they agree to abide.

newbie A newcomer. Used to describe a new user to the internet, or someone who has recently joined a particular online community

Notepad A simple text-editing program contained in Microsoft Windows

O

Office A widely-used suite of programs by Microsoft whose main components are Word (a word-processing program), Excel (a spreadsheet program), Access (a database program), PowerPoint (a presentation program) and Office (an email and calendar program).

offline Not connected to the internet. A user might perform some work offline such as writing and saving emails, then go online in order to complete another task such as sending them.

online Connected to the internet or a specific network

online conference A community of people communicating online for a particular purpose, usually replicating a face-to-face conference to some extent. An online conference may meet/communicate in real time using synchronous tools (e.g. chat, live audio and/or video), or asynchronous tools over an extended period of time

open-source Open-source software enables any user with the necessary knowledge to make changes to the source code and then re-distribute it if desired. Open-source software may incur a fee depending on the distributor, but may also be free. One of the best known open-source softwares is the operating system Linux.

operators characters used when performing a search in order to refine/define further a particular search (e.g. in a search engine). For example, using a + symbol when searching on more than one word will yield results containing both words, whereas a - symbol used before a word will ensure that the results do not contain that word.

orphan page A web page with no links to enable navigation back to the rest of the website to which it belongs.

P

password A sequence of characters (usually numbers and letters) known only by a certain user which, in conjunction with a *username*, grants the user access to a computer, a network or another system. See also username.

PHP A popular open-source programming language used mostly for developing dynamic web content. Web pages written in PHP can interact with the web server, i.e. they can gather information from a user, database, or web page and then display dynamically produced web pages.

plain text A document or message sent in a format which supports only text, i.e. cannot include images or formatting options such as bold, italics or underline. Most email programs allow email messages to be created in plain text and in HTML or "rich text". Plain text messages are quicker to send but cannot include images or formatting.

point and click A solution which enables quick and simple setup of a program/page/site without any coding/programming being necessary.

portal A system which offers a user access to a number of programs/websites in one interface (e.g. on a website). Instead of having to open a number of programs, the user can access the portal and then go to each of a number of programs from there. Yahoo! is an example of an online portal.

post (also posting) A message sent to an email discussion group or web-based forum.

PowerPoint One of a number of programs contained in the Microsoft Office suite of programs. PowerPoint allows a user to create digital slides (normally for projection on a data projector), for use while giving a presentation.

Programs menu The list of programs that appears when clicking the Start - Programs sequence in Windows.

R

Registrar A company authorised to register domain-names for individual users or companies.

return The large key on the computer keyboard which (usually) allows a user to finalise input into the computer e.g. when entering data into an online form. It can also serve to insert line breaks in text-processing programs or HTML editors.

S

scroll To move up or down an electronic document using the mouse or the up/down arrow keys.

search engine A tool which allows a user to find information on a website, on the internet or on an intranet. Popular internet search engines include Google and AllTheWeb.

search terms The words or numbers used when performing a search on a *search engine*.

service provider (also known as Internet Service Provider or ISP) A company or institution that offers services including connection to the internet.

shareware Software which can be tried for free for a limited period of time, after which payment needs to be made in order to continue using it. See also *freeware*.

sound card A piece of hardware usually installed in a computer to allow it to play back and/or record sound.

source code The underlying code behind a computer program or web page, consisting of human-readable commands. In the case of a web page, the code is interpreted and displayed in a *browser* for a user.

spellcheck A feature commonly built into word-processing, email and other programs to automatically check the spelling of text a user enters.

spreadsheet A computer-based program commonly used for accounting or bookkeeping and consisting of sheets of grids. A user can enter text or numbers into the individual fields of the grids and specify functions to be performed between the different fields, such as adding up the contents of a particular column.

storage medium Any type of hardware that can be used for storing data. Examples are floppy disks, CDs, DVDs, Flash cards, USB memory sticks and more.

streamed A streamed audio or video file begins playing (almost) immediately once it has been accessed (by clicking on a link on a website, for example), rather than needing to be downloaded completely first.

subject line The field in an email which can be completed by the writer of an email to indicate to the recipient what the subject of the email is.

synchronous Live, or in real time. A synchronous tool allows immediate interaction between two or more users. Examples of synchronous tools are chat rooms, Instant Messaging programs, live audio/video conferencing and more. See also *asynchronous*.

System tray In Microsoft Windows, the area on a computer screen (normally in the bottom right hand corner of the desktop) showing the clock and other icons indicating programs or processes that are running permanently while the computer is turned on.

T

tag A formatting command used in HTML that causes a browser to display content in a certain way. The <b> tag for example causes the browser to display text in bold, while <i> causes the browser to display text in italics.

template A document containing standard formatting which can be applied to a large number of documents. A website for example may be built from a template, causing all pages of the website to have the same *look and feel*.

text chat A system that allows people connected to the internet to communicate with each other live via text-based messages. See also *chat*.

text editor A program such as *Notepad* which allows a user to write text. Text editors commonly do not have advanced formatting features such as bold, italic or underline, nor other features such as *spellchecks*.

thread A discussion forum is commonly made up of threads, each one being a conversation about a different topic or subject area.

TLD (Top-Level Domain) The final component of a domain-name, namely the part after the last dot in the address. For example, in the website address http://www.microsoft.com the TLD is 'com'.

Treasure Hunt A 'hunt' on the internet, planned by one person and followed by one or more others. Treasure Hunts might cause the participants to visit certain websites in order to gather certain information, become familiar with specific websites and so on. See also *WebQuest*.

U

URL Uniform Resource Locator. The unique website address for every page on the World Wide Web. URLs are commonly in the form http://www.domainname.com/page.html .

username A unique identifier for a certain user in a computer system. A username/password combination is used to allow an individual access to computer programs, networks or other applications.

V

video-conferencing (or **dedicated video-conferencing**) A system which makes use of a high-speed connection for high-quality video and sound communication between users in different locations.

virtual classroom An online system which replicates a face-to-face classroom. Virtual classrooms may be *synchronous* or *asynchronous* or combine elements of both, e.g. a file-sharing area, a chat room, a web-based forum and more.

Virtual Learning Environment (VLE) A system for developing and distributing online learning materials. A VLE may also contain class management features such as student tracking (to enable an instructor to see which pages of a course a student has visited), grade management and logging, and more. See also *course management system* and *learning management system*.

virus A program or piece of code which distributes itself from one computer to another one without the knowledge or consent of the computer user. Some viruses are fairly benign and do nothing other than continue to distribute themselves, while others affect the computer in any number of (usually harmful) ways.

W

web hosting company A company which maintains web servers in order to allow other companies or individuals to make their websites available on the WWW.

web page (also web page) A page written in *HTML* or another *browser*-readable language.

web presence A company or individual who has a website which can be accessed by other users on the WWW is said to have a web presence.

web server A computer permanently connected to the internet which stores one or more websites and makes them available on the WWW.

web space The amount of server-space (usually in *megabytes*) a user has available on a *web server*.

G

Glossary

webcam A camera attached to a computer which enables a users to record or send live video or still pictures.

weblog - see *blog*

WebQuest An activity in which one or more users (e.g. learners) gather information from the Internet according to criteria/guidelines set by e.g. an instructor. See also *Treasure Hunt*.

website A collection of web pages put together by a company, institution or individual. A website may promote an individual, a product or a company; offer information of some sort; contain activities of various kinds, and much more.

whisper The process of sending a private text message within an open chat room. Instead of all users being able to read the text message, when "whispering" only the designated recipient of the message can read it.

whiteboard A tool sometimes bundled with Internet conferencing software such as Microsoft NetMeeting which allows users to share a common screen. One participant can for example write or draw onto the whiteboard, with the new/changed content being visible immediately to all other meeting participants. A whiteboard can often be saved at any point during the meeting for future reference, or be prepared before a meeting and opened during it for sharing and collaborating.

WHOIS A service which allows a user to find details about the owner and administration of a particular domain name.

Wingdings A font supported by Microsoft Word and other programs consisting largely of symbols and icons.

word processor (also word-processing program) A software program designed for the manipulation and presentation of text. Microsoft Word is perhaps the best-known word processor.

World Wide Web (WWW) The set of documents and files accessible via the HTTP protocol on the internet.

WYSIWYG (What You See Is What You Get) A type of web page editor that produces HTML code for the user while displaying the page in the same way a browser will do. A WYSIWYG editor might be used by someone who wants to design a web page but has no knowledge of HTML. Popular WYSIWYG editors include Macromedia Dreamweaver and Adobe GoLive.

X

XML (Extensible Markup Language) A markup language which in turn can be used for creating other markup languages for specific purposes (e.g. for representing mathematical or chemical symbols). Markup languages created using XML are for example RSS, MathML and more. XML is also commonly used for transferring data between different programs or websites.

Index

address, 13
advantages of using IT, 8
assessment. *See* Content Management Systems
astrology, website topics, 30
audio, recording from the internet, 132
audio recording software, 131
audio/Video. *See* Internet audio/video conferencing
audio/video-conferencing
    dedicated, 70
    how to teach using, 76
    internet, 70
authoring software, 112
    Hot Potatoes, 113
    Quia, 117
basics of IT, 12
blended solution, 13
blogs, 140
browser, 13
business English CD-ROMs, 153
CD-ROMs, 49, 152
    incorporating into a course, 53
    practical considerations, 51
    using in the classroom, 56
    versus internet, 50
celebrities, website topics, 28
chat. *See* text-chat, Internet Relay Chat
chat rooms, 59
class, text chat, 64
classroom, using CD-ROMs, 56
company websites, website topics, 37

Index

concordancers, 121
    British National Corpus, 125
    Collins CoBuild, 124
    using, 127
    using a search engine, 129
    WordSmith Tools, 123
conferencing. *See* internet audio/video conferencing
    internet versus instant messaging, 71
content management, 83
content Management Systems, 84
copyright, 23
courses, incorporating CD-ROMs, 53
cracking the code, 25
discussion groups. See Email
domain name, 13, 108
e-learning, 13
email, 13
    address, 13
    discussion groups, 18
    homework and feedback, 16
    Hotmail, 15
    keeping students informed, 17
    managing, 19
    Outlook Express, 15
    proofreading students' documents, 17
    Student activities, 16
    using, 15
    Yahoo, 15
email activities
    information gathering, 16
    jigsaw activities, 17
    role plays, 17
    role plays, 17
English for academic purposes CD-ROMs, 154
exam preparation CD-ROMs, 154
explanations, website topics, 36
F2F. *See* face to face

Index

face-to-face, 13
feedback by email, 16
film, website topics, 29
food, website topics, 30
forums, 23
FTP, 105
gap-fills, 25
GeoCities, 103
history, website topics, 33
holidays, website topics, 33
homework by email, 16
Hot Potatoes, 113
HTML, 90
    alternatives, 100
    first steps learning, 92
hyperlinks, 13
information gap, 26
information-gathering, 16
Instant Messaging, 58, 61
    versus internet conferencing, 71
interactive exercises, 112, 119
internet, 12
    copyright, 23
    recording from the internet, 132
    versus CD-ROM, 50
internet audio/video conferencing, 70
internet conferencing
    integrating into your teaching, 78
    versus instant messaging, 71
Internet Relay Chat, 58, 61
InterNIC, 109
ISP, 109
IT
    advantages, 8
    basics, 12
    Why use IT, 8
jigsaw activities, 17

Index

jigsaw reading, 26
jobs, website topics, 32
keyboard shortcuts, 13
learning management systems, 81, 83
LMS. *See* Learning Management Systems
managing your emails, 19
messaging. *See* Instant Messaging
music topics, 27
netiquette, 18
NetMeeting, 73
network, 12
news, website topics, 35
poetry, website topics, 34
presentation software, 138
pronunciation CD-ROMs, 153
proofreading, 17
publicising websites, 110
publishers websites, 156
Quia, 117
reading comprehension, 26
reconstructing text, 25
reference works CD-ROMs, 154
role-plays, 17
romance and dating, website topics, 38
search engine, 21
    using as a concordancer, 129
software, 121
software concordancers, 121
sports, website topics, 37
spreadsheets, 136
student activities by email, 16
teachers' resources CD-ROMs, 154
teaching
    using internet audio/video conferencing, 76
    with text chat, 63
text-chat, 58
    in class, 64

Index

    limitations, 68
    teaching, 63
topics, 27
Tripod, 103
uniform resource locator. See URL
uploading, 105
URL, 13
using WebQuests, 45
web. *See* world wide web
web pages, 13
    uploading, 105
web server, 105
WebQuests, 40
    using, 45
website
    activities, 24
    addresses, 144
    creating your own, 89
    EFL/TESOL, 23
    exercises, 24
    publicising, 110
    topics, 27
website activities
    gap-fills, 25
    cracking the code, 25
    Information gap, 26
    jigsaw reading, 26
    reading comprehension, 26
    reconstructing text, 25
    word-completion, 25
website topics
    astrology and star signs, 30
    celebrities and famous people, 28
    company websites, 37
    explanations, 36
    film and music reviews, 29
    food, 30, 32

    history, 33
    holidays, 33
    music, 27
    news, 35
    poetry, 34
    romance and dating, 38
    sports, 37
websites
    for language teaching, 21
WHOIS, 109
word processor, 135
word-completion, 25
world wide web, 13
WWW. *See* world wide web

introduction

advantages of one-to-one lessons for the student

introduction

advantages of one-to-one lessons for the student

1

introduction

advantages of one-to-one lessons for the student

1

introduction

advantages of one-to-one lessons for the student

1

introduction

advantages of one-to-one lessons for the student

1

introduction

advantages of one-to-one lessons for the student

1

introduction

advantages of one-to-one lessons for the student

1

introduction

advantages of one-to-one lessons for the student

1

introduction

advantages of one-to-one lessons for the student

1

introduction